PERFECTED IN THE FAITH

SAINT SHENOUDA PRESS

UPPER ROOM MEDIA

PERFECTED IN THE FAITH

A Commemoration of His Saints

ST SHENOUDA PRESS
SYDNEY, AUSTRALIA
2020

Perfected in the Faith
St Mark's Coptic Church, Sydney, Australia

ST SHENOUDA PRESS
8419 Putty Rd,
Putty, NSW, 2330
Sydney, Australia

www.stshenoudapress.com

ISBN 13: 978-0-6488658-1-0

Cover Design:
Hani Ghaly,
Begoury Graphics
begourygraphics@gmail.com

Contents

Content

Introduction

"Therefore we also, since we are surrounded by so great a cloud of witnesses, let us lay aside every weight, and the sin which so easily ensnares us, and let us run with endurance the race that is set before us, looking unto Jesus, the author and finisher of our faith, who for the joy that was set before Him endured the cross, despising the shame, and has sat down at the right hand of the throne of God." - Hebrews 12:1-2

These verses are written by St Paul following the famed chapter listing the heroes of faith – faithful examples of those who fought the good fight, finished the race and kept the faith. (2 Timothy 4:7)

This 'cloud of witnesses' provide for us encouragement and proof. They encourage us through their model of faith, both their faults and their triumphs, giving proof of God's presence in their lives and of the possibility of us developing a similar relationship with Him here on earth.

We take this model of commemorating saints from Jesus Himself who says about the woman who anointed his feet at Bethany: 'Assuredly, I say to you, wherever this gospel is preached in the whole world, what this woman has done will also be told as a memorial to her' Matthew 26:13 The Commemoration of the Saints in the Liturgy serves to live out this purpose of providing a memorial of those who anointed the feet of Christ through the sweet offering of their lives. The purpose of this memorial as St Paul says is ultimately to help us to look 'unto Jesus' and His endurance of the cross and His ultimate victory, which He likewise promises to us.

For this reason the youth of St Mark's Coptic Orthodox Church (Sydney, Australia) have created this book detailing the lives of these saints. From biblical saints to patriarchs to monks, and everything in between, you will find in this book a detailed yet concise description of all these saints' lives and how they contributed to the church that we know and love today.

The Book of Acts, which chronicles the early life of the church, does not finish with the word 'amen' but is continued in the life of the Church, through her evangelical mission and the life of her saints providing a witness to the love of God through Jesus Christ. And so we must remember that the heroes of faith and the list of saints is not complete. You are called to be one of these saints. And just as the book of Acts does not finish with the word 'amen' – the final page of this book is intentionally left blank – for you, for your name, and for your life's story.

PART 1
Biblical Saints

THE VIRGIN SAINT MARY

Saint Mary was born to Saint Joachim (of the seed of David, of the tribe of Judah) and Saint Anna, righteous people who loved God, who had prayed to God for many years to be blessed with a child, vowing to dedicate her to the Temple of God. Having such faith in God, they were not only blessed with a child, but with the honour of having the mother of God as their child.

Saint Mary was taken to the Temple at the age of three and dedicated to God in fulfilment of her parents' promise. Her entrance into the Temple is commemorated on the 3rd day of the Coptic month of Kiahk.

At the age of twelve, she had to leave the Temple. She was placed in the care of Saint Joseph the Carpenter, but remained a virgin. While she was in the care of Saint Joseph, Archangel Gabriel came and announced the news of the Lord's conception and birth, but while remaining a virgin.

Saint Mary

Other Names Theotokos (Mother of God)

Birth 18BC

Feast Mesra 16/August 22 (assumption of her body),
Kiahk 3/December 12 (entrance into the Temple),
21st of every Coptic month (commemoration)

Famous Quote "Behold the maidservant of the Lord! Let it be to me according to your word."

Saint Bede highlights the Virgin's humility at the Annunciation of the Archangel Gabriel; *"St Mary teaches us how worthless she felt of herself and that she received, by the heavenly grace that was lavished on her, every sort of good merit that she had. She demonstrates that in her own judgment she was indeed Christ's humble handmaid, but with respect to heavenly grace she pronounces herself all at once lifted up and glorified to such a degree that rightly her pre-eminent blessedness would be marveled at by the voices of all nations"*

As soon as she hears about Saint Elizabeth's pregnancy, she so humbly goes to visit her, thinking of nothing else but helping her out in her time of need. She didn't stay home and wish to be served during her own pregnancy, but rather wished to serve her older cousin without complaint.

Saint Mary is best known by her undeniable precious response to Archangel Gabriel at the announcement of the birth of Christ through her. She says, *"Behold the maidservant of the Lord! Let it be to me according to your word"* (Luke 1:38). We occasionally underestimate the depth of this phrase, missing out on the true meaning it carries. St Mary makes a pledge here to God, dedicating herself as a handmaid of God, a slave by complete dedication - in body, soul and spirit. She consecrates her life to celibacy after this incredible revelation was made to her by Archangel Gabriel. She makes a testimony to the world that she will remain pure, and live completely for the Living God, having her heart entirely possessed by the Spirit of God, only beating for God most High. The handmaid of the Lord, became the Mother of the Lord, and yet remained a true servant, in total submission to

His will for all her days. She humbly accepts the Lord's will, effectively returning her soul to the time before Adam and Eve's fall and renounces their sin of rejecting the Living God. Becoming a slave to the love of God, she frees herself from the corruption of this world, and the chains of pride, through the indwelling purifying Word of God in her thoughts, heart and her very womb. Another story that was testament to Saint Mary's kindness and compassion was during the wedding of Cana of Galilee. As the story goes, *"And when they ran out of wine, the mother of Jesus said to Him, "They have no wine." Jesus said to her, "Woman, what does your concern have to do with Me? My hour has not yet come." His mother said to the servants, "Whatever He says to you, do it"* (John 2:3-5). Our Lord was obedient to His mother, Saint Mary, knowing her thoughts were set on those in need.

Our Lady, the Virgin, was so precious in the sight of our Lord, that when the time drew near for her departure, it was not fitting for her body to remain on earth. The Holy Spirit informed her of her coming departure while she was praying at the Holy Sepulchre. At the time of her departure, she lay in bed surrounded by the disciples, the virgins, the Saviour of the world Himself and thousands of thousands of heavenly hosts. He consoled her and informed her of the everlasting joy that awaited her. She stretched out her hands and blessed the disciples and virgins before her soul was taken into the heavens.

Her body was shrouded and carried to Gethsemane. Along the way, some Jews tried to stop the disciples from burying her body. The hands of one that seized her coffin became detached from his body. He repented of his evils deeds and immediately his hands were re-attached as they were before.

Saint Thomas was absent at the time of her departure. On his way back to Jerusalem, he saw angels carrying St Mary's precious body into the heavens. One of the angels said to him, *"Hurry and kiss the pure body of St Mary."* When he arrived, he informed the disciples of what he had seen. The disciples were in disbelief and took him to the tomb where they had laid her body. They found the tomb was empty.

The Holy Spirit told them, *"The Lord did not Will to leave Her Holy body on earth."* The Lord promised His disciples that they would see her in the flesh another time. This was fulfilled on the 16th day of the month. On the 16th, they saw Saint Mary sitting on the right hand of God.

Saint Mary lived sixty years on earth; twelve years in the Temple, thirty years in the house of Joseph and fourteen years at the care of St John the Beloved of our Saviour. The assumption of her body is commemorated on 16th day of the Coptic month of Mesra. She is also commemorated on the 21st of every Coptic month.

Saint John the Baptist

John the Baptist was born to Zechariah the priest and Elizabeth, who was the cousin of Saint Mary, during the time of Herod king of Judea. They were both righteous in the sight of God, but had no children of their own despite their old age.

One day, when Zechariah's lot fell to burn incense, he went into the Temple of the Lord, and the Archangel Gabriel appeared to him, saying, *"Do not be afraid, Zacharias, for your prayer is heard; and your wife Elizabeth will bear you a son, and you shall call his name John."* Because he did not believe the angel, Zechariah became mute until the day of John's circumcision, when he opened his mouth and prophesied, *'you, child, will be called the prophet of the Highest; for you will go before the face of the Lord to prepare His ways.'"*
- Luke 1:57-76

St John the Baptist

Other Names the Forerunner

Birth Paona 13/June 20 (birth)

Feast Tout 2/September 12 (martyrdom)

Famous Quote "I baptize with water, but there stands One among you whom you do not know. It is He who, coming after me, is preferred before me, whose sandal strap I am not worthy to loose." – John 1:26-27

When John was two years old, King Herod wrote a decree that ordered all children under the age of three years old to be put to death, in fear of the prophecies of the birth of Christ. Zechariah took the child and laid him on the altar of the sanctuary and told the soldiers, *"I have received him from this place."* The angel of the

Lord caught up the child and brought him to the desert of Ziphana. The enraged soldiers then killed his father Zechariah (some including Origen have suggested that for this reason the Lord had said to the Jews: *"That on you may come all the righteous blood shed on the earth, from the blood of righteous Abel to the blood of Zechariah, son of Berechiah, whom you murdered between the Temple and the altar"* (Matthew 23:35).

The gospel of Saint Luke tells us that *"the young child John grew and became strong in spirit in the desert, till the day of his manifestation to Israel"* (Luke 1:80).

John became an example of asceticism for generations till now. Saint Matthew tells us that he was clothed in camel's hair, with a leather belt, and ate locusts and wild honey. He persevered in prayers in the wilderness, until the Lord sent him to go out before Christ, and preach and bear witness to Him (hence his title is, 'the forerunner').

Saint John did not waver from his mission to preach the baptism of repentance. He went out throughout Judea saying, *"Repent for the kingdom of heaven is at hand,"* and many, throughout all Judea and the surrounding regions, went to be baptised by him in the Jordan.

Our Lord Jesus Christ Himself came from Galilee to be baptised by John. Whilst John was trying to prevent Him, saying, *"I have need to be baptised by You,"* Jesus answered, *"Permit it to be so now, for thus it is fitting for us to fulfil all righteousness."* After Jesus had been baptised, the heavens were opened to Him and he saw the Spirit of God descending like a dove upon Him, and a voice came from heaven saying, *"This is My Beloved Son, in whom I am well pleased."*

John became a model of servitude in self-denial and selflessness, and clothed in all humility. When his disciples came, and reported that people were leaving him and following Jesus, he said this joy of his was fulfilled, and that *"He must increase but I must decrease."*

Saint John showed great boldness and zeal. He even went to the extent of admonishing Herod Antipas, the son of Herod the great, for marrying Herodias (who was the wife of Herod's brother). Herod imprisoned John for over a year, however was afraid to kill him. At that time, John's disciples frequently visited him, and he did not neglect his duties to them.

During the celebration of Herod's birthday, the daughter of Herodias danced before them and this pleased Herod. He promised to give her anything she asked for to show his gratitude. At the advice of her mother, she asked for the head of John the Baptist to be brought on a platter. Although he was remorseful, Herod ordered the beheading of John the Baptist.

During the beheading, it was said that his voice cried out saying, *"It is not right for you to take your brother's wife."* His disciples took his body and buried it, and when Jesus heard it, He departed from the people and went alone into a deserted place (Matthew 14:2-13).

His martyrdom took place at the end of the 31st or 32nd year of Christ. Saint John the Baptist is said to be sitting at the right hand of God, with a purity that can be compared only to the angels in heaven. His birth is commemorated on the 13th day of the Coptic month of Paona and his martyrdom is commemorated on the 2nd day of the Coptic month of Tout.

SAINT STEPHEN THE ARCHDEACON

Saint Stephen the archdeacon is a blessed figure in Christianity and the Coptic Church, who established a reputation for his abundant courage, faith and defence of our Lord. These virtues eventually led to his martyrdom by stoning – affirming his title as the first martyr of the church. Unfortunately, little is documented regarding the numerous wonders and signs he performed among the people, yet he earns the distinction of consecutive Biblical chapters (Acts 6 & 7) detailing his trial and death.

In approximately 34 AD, just after Christ's death and resurrection, the number of Christians and disciples of the Lord multiplied greatly. There arose complaints and issues as particular groups

St Stephen the Archdeacon

Other Names The protomartyr, the first martyr

Birth 5AD

Feast Toba 1/January 9 (martyrdom)

Tout 15/ September 25 (translocation of Relics)

Famous Quote "Look! I see the heavens opened and the Son of Man standing at the right hand of God!"

were neglected in church distributions. The twelve disciples became aware of this issue and summoned the multitude of these followers, commanding them to choose seven men among them *of good reputation, full of the Holy Spirit and wisdom"* (Acts 6:3) to help the twelve. Of these seven, Saint Stephen was chosen – known as a man full of faith and the Holy Spirit.

He whole-heartedly assumed his role as an archdeacon, full of faith and power, performing many (undocumented) *"great wonders and signs among the people"* (Acts 6:8). His reputation developed and Jews arose from the Synagogue of the Freedman (Cyrenians, Alexandrians, and those from Cilica and Asia) who envied and they disputed with him. They were unable to refute the wisdom and the Spirit by which he spoke, so they resorted to secretly persuading false witnesses to speak against him.

The false witnesses spoke of Saint Stephen saying, *"We have heard him speak blasphemous words against Moses and God" (Acts 6:10)*. The Jews then stirred up the people, the elders and the scribes; and they came upon Saint Stephen and brought him to the council of the Jews to be put to trial. The false witnesses spoke again, saying, *"The man does not cease to speak blasphemous words against this holy place and the law" (Acts 6:13)*. Despite this, those who sat in the council looked upon Saint Stephen and saw the face of an angel.

Saint Stephen was further questioned by the high priest in the council, regarding the accusations of the false witnesses. What ensued from Saint Stephen is one of the most courageous, faithful and spirited speeches delivered in the Bible. He disproved their doubt regarding his faith; detailing the history from Abraham to Moses: the coming out of Abraham from Haran, the birth and the circumcision of Isaac, Jacob and his sons and their selling of Joseph, and how Joseph revealed himself to his brothers. He continued to narrate to them all the events until the building of the Temple.

To conclude his prominent speech, Saint Stephen upholds his virtue of courage and faith, calling the council *"Stiff-necked and circumcised in heart and ears!"* *(Acts 7:51)*. He continued, *"You always resist the Holy Spirit; as your fathers did, so do you. Which of the prophets did your fathers not persecute? And they killed those who foretold the coming of the Just One, of whom you now have become the betrayers and murderers, who have received the law by the direction of angels and have not kept it." (Acts 7:52-53)*. It is this speech that defines the virtue of bravery in Saint Stephen's life, and provided his prosecutors with the impetus to pursue their attack.

It is written, *"When they heard these things they were cut to the heart, and they gnashed at him with their teeth." (Acts 7:54)*. Once again Saint Stephen's holiness and blessing of the Holy Spirit shone through and he gazed into heaven and saw the glory of God, and Jesus standing at His right hand. He said, *"Look! I see the heavens opened and the Son of Man standing at the right hand of God!" (Acts 7:56)*. The council and those that were stirred then cried out with a loud voice, stopped their ears, and ran at him together.

Saint Stephen was cast out of the city and stoned to martyrdom. Very interestingly, the witnesses and those that stoned Saint Stephen *"laid down their clothes at the feet of a young man named Saul" (Acts 7:58)*. This young man Saul, who witnessed and was involved in many martyrdoms, became Saint Paul – writer and author of most of the books in the Bible, and the most famous preacher of Christianity.

As Saint Stephen was stoned, he called on God and said *"Lord Jesus, receive my spirit."* He then knelt down and cried out with a loud voice, *"Lord, do not charge them with this sin."* And when he had said this, he fell asleep. This is testament to his forgiveness and compassion, virtues that were clear throughout his life.

Saint Stephen is venerated as a saint in both Oriental and Eastern Orthodox churches, as well as the Catholic and Anglican churches. The name Stephen is originally derived from the Greek name *Stepahnos* meaning 'crown.' The symbolism of his name is a stark reminder of the crown of martyrdom he pioneered. Aptly, in Coptic iconography, he is depicted with numerous stones, to remind us of the brutal death he experienced.

The Coptic Church celebrates the death and martyrdom of Saint Stephen on the 1st of Toba each year.

After his departure, Saint Stephen appeared several times to a priest named Lucianus, telling him his name and where his body was buried. Lucianus informed the bishop of Jerusalem of the place revealed in his sleep. He went with two other bishops and dug up the ground, and a mighty earthquake took place. The coffin wherein the holy body was lying was revealed with sweet and precious aromas coming out from it. They heard voices of angels praising God saying *"Glory to God in the highest and on earth peace, good will toward men"*. The bishops carried his body praising with hymns and songs, and kept it in the church of Saint Stephen in Jerusalem.

The man who built this church died several years later, and his wife decided to bury him by the side of Saint Stephen's coffin. Eight years later she moved to Constantinople and mistakenly took Saint Stephen's coffin with her instead of her husband's. The ship wherein she travelled was blessed, and the coffin produced songs and praises during the trip. She examined the coffin to find Saint Stephen's body, and this was the will of God. She informed the emperor of Constantinople of what happened and he rose with the Archbishop and priests to move the coffin to the royal palace. The ship and royal palace were blessed with many signs.

The Emperor laid the holy body on two mules to be carried to the royal palace, and when they came to a place called Constantinious the mules stopped. They were beaten but refused to move, and the words, *"It is meet to place the Saint here"* come out of one of their mouths. All marvelled, and the Emperor ordered a church to be built for Saint Stephen. The translocation of his body is commemorated on the 15th of the Coptic month of Tout.

Saint Mark

Saint Mark was born in Cyrene, one of the cities of Pentopolis, approximately 15 years after the birth of Christ. Being born of Jewish parents, his father's name was Aristopolis and his mother's Mary. Their family migrated to Palestine to avoid barbarian attacks. While there, they met Christ and played a crucial role in His time on earth. Mary followed Christ from the beginning of His ministry: she, as well as Saint Mark, were present at the wedding of Cana of Galilee, and continued with Him until the end of His ministry. The upper room of her house is considered to be the first church as it hosted the last supper of our Lord Jesus Christ. Even after Jesus' death, Mary and Mark were one of the few that remained faithful to Christ, and gathered the disciples together in the upper room of their house till the day of Pentecost.

Being at the forefront of our Lord's ministry, Saint Mark was hand-picked as one of the 70 apostles who went out to the nations and evangelised. Saint Mark was arguably one of the most suited for evangelizing at his

Saint Mark

Other Names The Apostle, Evangelist, Martyr and First Pope of Alexandria.

Feast Baramouda 13/April 26 (martyrdom)

Paouna 15/June 22 (return of relics),

Paouna 17/June 24 (arrival of the relics to the Cathedral of St Mark)

Famous Quote "Do not become a disciple of one who praises himself, in case you learn pride instead of humility"

time, as he was taught by both Saint Peter (in Judea), and Saint Paul (in Antioch), as well as being taught directly by Christ up until the point of His crucifixion (he was the man that left his linen cloth and fled when they were apprehending Jesus). After some contention that arose with Saint Paul, humbly, he did not go with him on his second missionary trip but rather went with Barnabas and began his own mission journey in Cyprus. After going back home to Pentopolis, Saint Mark was directed by the Holy Spirit and succeeded in establishing the church in Egypt.

Throughout Saint Mark's extensive missionary, we see his total trust and reliance on Christ. Particularly, entering Egypt alone at that time was dangerous and an audacious undertaking. It was arguably the world's strongest philosophical country, that housed the school of Alexandria, and was predominantly a pagan nation. Upon his arrival in Egypt, the Lord sent him Ananias as a helper. When the strap of Saint Mark's sandal had ripped, he approached Ananias the shoemaker for repair. As he was sowing his sandal, Ananias pierced his finger and screamed out, '*Oh the One God.*' Seen as an opportunity then to present Christ, Saint Mark healed him and preaches Jesus, who is the "One God." Ananias and his family hastily accept the faith and were baptized.

The Evangelist Mark is considered as the founder and first pope of the Coptic Orthodox church, and is responsible for establishing the See of Alexandria. It is said that just the mere presence of Saint Mark in Egypt abolished the idols of the land. The name of Christ quickly spread throughout Egypt through Saint Mark's works and preaching. He consequently ordained

Ananias as a Bishop, and with him seven priests and deacons. The pagan mob quickly rose in anger against this new 'Way,' so Saint Mark fled from Alexandria and joined Saint Peter and Saint Paul in Rome, in which he remained ministering to them until their martyrdom in 64 AD.

One of the most notable stories involving the Evangelist takes place when he and his father were travelling across the desert to the Jordan. On their journey a fierce lion, and lioness encountered them and sought to devour them. Saint Mark's father, fearing the lions, begged his son to run away and flee while he distracted the beast and awaited his fate. Rather than running, Saint Mark displayed seemingly irrational faith in Christ, and calmly began praying while standing firm in the presence of the lions. He made the sign of the Cross over himself first and then over the attacking lions. Suddenly the two animals split in half and because of that miracle his father immediately believed in the Lord Jesus Christ and was baptized.

For this reason, and for being a symbol of strength and honour, Saint Mark has ever since been symbolized by the figure of a lion. The people of Venice who consider him as their intercessor, chose to build a statue of a winged lion at Saint Mark's square to give them strength and protection. This statue remains there till this day.

After the martyrdom of Saint Paul and Saint Peter in 67 AD, Saint Mark returned to the church he established in Alexandria to find that the people had multiplied in numbers and built many churches. It is believed that at this time he wrote the first Gospel -the Gospel according to St Mark, which was written to the Romans. Presenting Christ as a king full of strength and power, this not only acted as a call for the Romans at the time, but also revolutionized the early church. It is believed that Saint Mathew and Saint Luke used this gospel to write their own, and it also served as the foundation for the Christian belief.

Shortly after, the devil stirred up the rulers of Egypt against Saint Mark, they rushed forward to the sanctuary and seized him. They tortured him on many different accounts; by fastening a rope around his neck and dragging him with a horse around the city, screaming 'drag the serpent through the cattle shed'. In response, the saint in the midst of his torture continued as a beacon of evangelism by praising God saying, *'Thanks be to thee O Lord because Thou hast made me worthy to suffer for thy Holy name."* They did this for many days, until an angel appeared to Saint Mark and comforted him and foretold of his glorified position in heaven. That same day, the saint's flesh was lacerated and he received the crown of martyrdom.

Due to his steadfast and strong zeal for our Lord, Saint Mark successfully evangelized in the most stubborn and strongest of cities. His steadfast and strong faith in the cross of Christ were pivotal to his God-given ability to calm two wild beasts as a youth. His steadfast and strong loyalty to the King compelled him to face death without fear and say, *'thanks be to thee, O Lord.'* His martyrdom is commemorated on the 13th day of the Coptic month of Baramouda.

On the 15th day of the Coptic month of Paona, the returning of his relics is commemorated. In 1968, during the reign of Pope Kyrillos VI, the relics of the great Saint Mark that were kept in Rome by the Roman Pope of that time were carried back to Egyptian land. When the plane landed in Egypt, Pope Kyrillos VI retrived the relics from the plane. The flight had been delayed till night time. Despite this, three white doves were seen by spectators to fly over the plane. This was a strange sight since birds do not fly at night and they were notably bright for all spectators to see. Some believe these birds were the heavenly hosts welcoming the relics of this great saint back to the land of Egypt. Pope Kyrillos carried the relics to the Cathedral of Saint Mark and consecrated the altar in the name of Saint Mark. The arrival of the relics of Saint Mark at the Cathedral is commemorated on the 17th day of the Coptic month of Paona.

PART 2
THE PATRIARCHS

SAINT SEVERUS THE PATRIARCH

Saint Severus was born in Sozopolis, Pisidia to Christian parents in 465 AD. His father was a senator and his grandfather, also named Severus, was Bishop of Sozopolis and attended the Council of Ephesus. Saint Severus was named after his grandfather when it was revealed in a vision to his father that, *"your son will strengthen orthodoxy, and his name will be after your name."*

In 485 AD, he travelled to Alexandria, Egypt where he studied grammar, rhetoric and philosophy. He became acquainted with Zacharias of Mytilene who introduced him to the works of Saint Gregory of Nazianzus and Saint Basil. While studying, it is said that Severus, along with Zacharias found a hoard of pagan idols and destroyed them in Menouthis.

St Severus the Patriarch

Other Names Severus the Great, Severus of Gaza

Birth ~465 AD

Feast Amshir 1/February 8 (departure)
Baba 2/October 12 (arrival in Egypt)
Kiahk 10/December 19 (relocation of his body)

Famous Quote "Let us make an enquiry of the divinity and humanity. They are not only different in everything but they are removed from each other and distinct as well. But when the union is professed from the two of them, the difference, again, in the quality of the natures from which there is the One Christ is not suppressed, but in conjunction by hypostasis division is driven out."

In 486 AD, he travelled to Phoenicia and studied law and philosophy. In his free time, he became interested in studying the Fathers of the Church. He grew in love for the church and was convinced he wanted to be baptised. In those days, it was a Pisidian custom that men could not be baptised until they had grown a beard. He was allowed baptism in year 488 AD in the Church of Saint Leontius at Tripolis.

Saint Severus led an ascetic life, rejecting bathing and pursued fasting. He left his studies and became a monk at the monastery of Peter the Iberian near Palestine as a monk. He remained there for several years. He remained in the desert until the year 500 AD when he became ill and returned to the Monastery of Saint Romanus in Maiuma.

At the Monastery of Saint Romanus, he was ordained a priest. He later received his inheritance from his parents. He donated most of his share to the poor and built a monastery.

One day when he was walking outside the city, he met a hermit who called out to him saying, "*welcome to you, Severus, teacher of Orthodoxy, and Patriarch of Antioch.*" The hermit prophesied what was to become of Severus.

In 508 AD, Nephalius wrote a defence of the Council of Chalcedon. Severus responded in his famous *Orationes ad Nephalium.* During the same time, Patriarch Elias of Jerusalem sent Nephalius with a decree to expel non-Chalcedonian monks from Palestine. Saint Severus was sent to Constantinople to defend the faith before Emperor Anastasias.

Alongside 200 non-Chalcedonian monks, Severus met with the Emperor and immediately gained favour in his sight. The Patriarch attempted to sway Anastasias to support the Council of Chalcedon through excerpts from Saint Cyril of Alexandria. In retaliation, Saint Severus wrote *Philalethes* to refute the work of Saint Cyril that had been taken out of context.

While in Constantinople, Saint Severus befriended Julian, Bishop of Halicarnasus. In 510, Anastasius allowed the return of non-Chalcedonians to their monasteries, followed by a ruling from the Emperor that adopted non-Chalcedonian interpretation of the *Heotikon* as law. Macedonius was deposed and replaced by Timothy I, a non-chalcedonian. Severus returned to his monastery in Palestine in 511 AD.

In 512 AD, Flavian II, Patriarch of Antioch was deposed by Anastasius and a synod was held at Laodicea in Syria to choose a successor. St Severus was chosen as Patrirach of Antioch. Upon his consecration, the baths of the palace were destroyed and the cooks were dismissed.

Between 514 and 518 AD, Saint Severus was accused of hiring Jewish mercenaries to kill 250 Chalcedonian pilgrims along with the monks that protected their bodies. John of Caesarea, wrote a defence of the Council of Chalcedon in response to St Severus' *Philalethes*.

After the death of Anastasius, he was succeeded by Emperor Justin I in 518 AD. Following advice from Chalcedonian bishops, Justin demanded Severus to affirm the Council of Chalcedon. Saint Severus refused and the Emperor thus ordered for his tongue to be cut off. The wife of his nephew, Saint Theodora found out about the order and warned Severus. Severus fled to Alexandria from Antioch by boat where he was received by Pope Timothy III of Alexandria. The Coptic Church celebrates his arrival on the 2nd day of the Coptic month of Baba.

While in Egypt, he performed numerous miracles and wrote three books against John of Caesarea in 519 AD. Julian of Halicarnassus exchanged letters with Severus regarding the body of Christ. Julian argued that the body of Christ was incorruptible and Severus argued that it was corruptible.

In 536 AD, a synod led by Menas declared the excommunication of Severus and all his books were banned. Severus fled to Constantinople with the aid of Empress Theodora and returned to Egypt. He remained in Sakha until his death on February 8, 538 AD. His departure is commemorated on the 1st day of the Coptic month of Amshir. His body was moved to Zogag Monastery and the relocation is celebrated on the 10th day of the Coptic month of Kiahk.

SAINT DIOSKOROS

Saint Dioskoros I was the 25th Pope of Alexandria. He is known as St Dioskoros the Great as well as The Champion of Orthodoxy because of his zeal for the Orthodox faith. He held the chair of the Pope of Alexandria from 444 AD to 451 AD.

Saint Dioskoros was a disciple and personal secretary of Saint Cyril of Alexandria. He served as the dean of the Catechetical School of Alexandria and accompanied Saint Cyril to the third ecumenical council held at Ephesus in 431 AD. He succeeded Saint Cyril as the Patriarch of the See of Alexandria.

St Dioskoros

Other Names Saint Dioskoros the Great, The Champion of Orthodoxy

Feast Tout 7/ September 17 (departure)

Saint Dioskoros walked in the footsteps of many great patriarchs through the three Eucemenical councils. The Patriarchs of Alexandria were highly respected for their theological contributions in the early centuries of Christianity. The Alexandrian See helped formulate and establish Christian dogma which is attested by the fact that the first three Christian Ecumenical councils (Nicea, Constantinople and Ephesus) were all presided over by Egyptian patriarchs.

It is this theologically competent pedigree, with its major foundational contributions to the Christian faith that moulded and influenced Saint Dioskoros' character, belief structure and uncompromising commitment to the truth. His close ties and exposure to Saint Cyril, one of Christian history's most prominent thinkers and eloquent writers cannot be underestimated in its influence on his character.

In the year 444 AD, within three months of his repose, Saint Cyril was succeeded by Saint Dioskoros as the 25th Patriarch of the See of Alexandria. It is with almost 400 years of proud theological influence that St Dioskoros began his ministry as the head of the See of Alexandria. He proved very quickly that he was a courageous leader that would fight for the Orthodox faith no matter what the consequence. He was the embodiment of the words written by King David many centuries earlier, "zeal for Your house has eaten me up."

Saint Dioskoros' passion and zeal for the Orthodox truth was quickly tested with a heresy promoted by Eutyches, an aged and respected head of a monastery of 300 monks in Constantinople. Eutyches preached that Jesus did not have a human body like ours, but rather a divine body – fully God, but not fully man. As a result, a local council was held by Flavian, the Patriarch of Constantinople in 448 AD to determine what would be done about this Eutychan controversy. After much questioning and examination, the council excommunicated Eutyches and deposed him from both his monastery and his priesthood.

However, Eutyches had an influential ally that was Leo, the Pope of Rome. Leo sent a letter to Eutyches praising his zeal in defending the true faith against the Nestorian Heresy. To add to this, after the determination of the council, Eutyches went over his patriarch Flavian's head and appealed directly to Emperor Theodosius, pleading his innocence.

Upon hearing about this new controversy from both Leo and Eutyches, Emperor Theodosius called a general council. As with previous councils the Emperor asked the Patriarch of Alexandria, in this case Saint Dioskoros, to preside over the council in Ephesus, the same city where his holy father Saint Cyril the Great presided over the third ecumenical council eighteen years earlier. A letter from the Emperor was circulated to all bishops asking them to attend the council that would start promptly on 1 August, 449 AD.

One hundred and thirty five bishops convened in Ephesus in order to reassess the sentence passed on Eutyches by the Flavian council. Eutyches was called up to state his current position on the nature of Christ. Upon hearing his declaration of faith the assembled bishops, including Saint Dioskoros, found it completely orthodox. Whether this was indeed his true belief was unknown. Eutyches called his previous position a misunderstanding. He was then declared orthodox and was unanimously acquitted and reinstated as a priest and the head of his monastery. As a result, the council condemned and excommunicated the seven bishops, including Flavian that had previously accused Eutyches.

Saint Dioskoros now had a growing list of enemies to which seven bishops were added. He fell out of favour with Pope Leo who had publically supported Eutyches' previous stand and was opposed to the council and its conclusions. *"Throughout this council St Dioskoros did not speak an evil word against Rome, while Leo in his epistles* refers to our Pope as *"that Egyptian plunderer", and 'the preacher of the devil's errors', who tried to force 'his villainous blasphemies' on his brethren."* Pope Leo then wrote a letter to the Emperor demanding that another council be called to correct the actions of what he called the "Dioskorian" council. Theodosius rejected his request.

Upon the death of Theodosius his power-hungry sister Pulcheria who was at the time a consecrated nun, broke her vows of celibacy and married a man called Marcianus so her husband could become Emperor. However, she could not find any bishops to bless her marriage. Pope Dioskoros and his bishops were most vocal in condemning her sinful act. However, for a political end, Pope Leo blessed their marriage when no other bishops would.

Again because of his righteousness and his love for the truth Saint Dioskoros' persecutors and persecutions increased. Where the previous Emperor was his supporter, the new Emperor and his wife were now vehemently against him.

Pope Leo saw his opportunity to strike and again asked the Emperor to hold another council. His request was this time granted and a council that would be attended by six hundred and thirty bishops was called in Chalcedon in 451 AD.

The plot against Saint Dioskoros, led by the now politically aligned Pope Leo, began immediately. He was accused of the same heresy of Eutyches along with many other false accusations. A letter from Pope Leo was read that stated, *"...Christ, Son, Lord, Only-begotten, known in two natures...."* Under pressure many of the bishops agreed, however Saint Dioskoros would not accept this statement which he considered heresy even if he had to suffer and die.

St Dioskoros was consequently exiled to the island of Gangra where he suffered many terrible things for his faith. At one point, they plucked out his beard and knocked out his teeth but rather than complain the he was accused unfairly and mistreated, he sent the hair from his beard and his broken teeth to his church in Alexandria with the words, *"this is the fruit of faith."*

Even when in exile the Lord honoured him by performing many miracles through his hands. After three years of suffering wrongfully for his unshakable faith in Gangra, he passed over to his loving Lord and undoubtedly heard the words, "well done, good and faithful servant." His death is commemorated on 7th day of the Coptic month of Tout.

SAINT ATHANASIUS THE APOSTOLIC

St Athanasius was the 20th Pope of Alexandria. He was born to pagan parents between the years of 295 and 298 A.D. He was Patriarch for 45 years and in that time, he fought relentlessly against Arian heresy, enduring 5 exiles. This earnt him the title of, "Athanasius against the world."

While Athanasius was still in school he saw some young Christian children amusing themselves by acting out a play of Christian rituals. One was playing bishop, some were deacons and some were priests. When he asked if he could play with them, they told him that he couldn't because he was Pagan. He answered them saying, "I am from

St Athansius the Apostolic

Other Names St Athanasius, Pope of Alexandria, Athanasius Against the world

Birth ~ 295-298 AD

Feast Bashons 7/ May 15 (departure)
Tout 13/ October 10 (miracle)

Famous Quote "For of what use is existence to the creature of it cannot know its Maker? How could men be reasonable beings if they had no knowledge of the Word and reason of the Father, through whom they had received their being? They would be no better than the beasts, had they no knowledge of earthly things; and why should God have made them at all, if He had not intended them to know Him? But, in fact, the good God has given them a share of His own image - that is in Our Lord Jesus Christ -and has made even themselves after the same image and likeness.

now on a Christian." They rejoiced greatly and made him pope in their play.

Pope Alexandros who was Pope at that time, passed by Athanasius and the other children and said to those who were with him that, "*this child [Athanasius] would be in a great position one day.*"

After the death of Athanasius' father, Athanasius and his mum were baptised by Pope Alexandros and taught the principles of the Christian faith. He remained close to the Pope, even giving all his money to the poor. He was made his personal secretary. After the departure of Pope Alexandros, Athanasius was chosen patriarch on May 5, 328 AD. Knowing that Pope Alexandros would recommend him as Pope, he hid in the mountains believing himself to be unworthy. The people eventually sought him out and brought him before the bishops to ordain him as Pope.

It was Pope Athanasius who ordained the first Metropolitan of Ethiopia, uniting the church of Ethiopia with the church of Alexandria.

During his reign, Arian heresy arose. According to Arius, Christ was *similar* to the Father but was not divine. Saint Athanasius argued and proclaimed in the creed, "*One in essence with the Father.*" This ultimately led to his enmity by followers of Arius.

Arius was excommunicated from Alexandria as a result. Having written a flattering and misleading letter to Emperor Constantine, Athanasius was pushed to allow Arius to return. Athanasius would not be persuaded and refused. In retaliation, the Arians accused Athanasius of four charges;

• That he supported Philominus who rebelled against the government

• That he broke the communion cup and destroyed the altar of the Eskira the priest

• That he killed bishop Arsanius and used his arms in sorcery

• That he raped a nun.

Pope Athanasius was cleared against the first charge. When a council was assembled to discuss the second charge, the priest Eskira's heart was moved and he revoked his false accusations. The Arians brought in the arms of a dead man and claimed them to be the arms of Bishop Arsanius. Meanwhile, Bishop Aransius was alive in a hidden room. Driven by regret, Arsanius entered the room to clear Athanasius of the false accusation. The Arians were enraged and claimed that Athanasius reattached his arms using sorcery.

A harlot was brought to testify falsely against Athanasius. Timothy the priest, one of Pope Athanasius' entourage, said to her, *"How dare you say that I came to your house and overpowered your will?"* The harlot, being unaware of which one Athanasius was, said, *"you are the one."* This exposed the fourth and final false accusation against Athanasius.

The Arians then prevented Athanasius from meeting with the Emperor, resulting in his exile despite the amelioration of all false claims. On February 5, 335 AD, Athanasius was exiled to France.

Soon after, Arius died a horrible death that was believed to have occurred as a punishment of divine justice. When the Emperor heard of Arius' death, he recognised Athanasius' innocence and allowed him to return to Alexandria in the year 337AD.

The Arians remained at large, and in 340AD, they assembled a council to excommunicate Athanasius once more and appointed Gregory in his place. This horrified the people of Alexandria and they tried to resist but this only caused the Arians to attack the churches of Alexandria on Good Friday, raping and killing many.

Pope Athanasius travelled to Rome and assembled a council to declare;

• His innocence

• The Cannons and the Creed of the faith as per the Council of Nicea

• Excommunication of Arian bishops

• Depose Gregory from his office

While this was occurring, Egyptian radicals rose to power and killed Gregory in 349 AD. Two bishops were delegated to meet with Emperor Constans, ruler of Italy who agreed to Athanasius' requests and gave orders in his favour.

The Arians decided to wait until the death of Emperor Constans and then accuse Athanasius of collaborating with Magneutius, enemy of the Emperor Constantius, the successor of Emperor Constans. When they did so, Constantius ordered soldiers to raid the Church of St Mary where St Athanasius was praying vespers. However, they were unable to recognise him among the people and the lamps were extinguished. As a result, Athanasius escaped to the desert for six years. The Arians appointed George of Cappadocia to take over but the Orthodox refused to accept him. George took over the churches and its properties and persecuted many. Saint Athanasius pleaded with Emperor Constantinus to either kill him or allow him to return to his rightful position as Patriarch. Constantinus ordered his men to put Athanasius on a small boat without food or water. After three days and smooth sailing under the care of the Lord, Saint Athanasius arrived in Alexandria. He was received by the believers with rejoicing and songs of praise. They brought him to the church and expelled George. This miracle is commemorated on the 13th day of the Coptic month of Tout.

After the death of Constantius, Julian became Emperor. He wished to unite the people of Alexandria so he returned Athanasius in 362 AD. After Athanasius arranged a council that made conditions for the return of Arians to the faith and gave attention to the preaching of pagans. This displeased Julian, who ordered the arrest of Athanasius.

Athanasius travelled to Upper Egypt. The Governor attempted to follow him but Athanasius remained hidden. Those around the Pope were greatly saddened by his exile, he comforted them saying that the persecution by Emperor Julian would pass by. While this conversation was occurring, there was news that

Julian was killed in war against the Persians. His final words were said to be, "You *have overcome me, O you son of Mary.*" It is believed that Abu Sefain was responsible for his death.

Julian was succeeded by Jovian, Jovian was succeeded by Valens. Valens was an Arian who ordered the exile of Athanasius for a fifth and final time in 367 AD. While Athanasius was in exile, the Emperor ordered 30 bishops to be killed for their support of Pope Athanasius. The Copts remained determined to keep their faith and Valens eventually lifted the persecution and returned Athanasius to his Chair in 368 AD.

During his reign, Athanasius did not fail to fight against Arian heresy, writing several books and solidifying the Coptic Orthodox Creed. "On the Incarnation" is one of his most notable works.

In 373 AD, at the age of 72, and 45 years on the Apostolic Throne, Pope Athanasius departed in peace. His departure is commemorated on the 7th day of Coptic month of Bashons.

SAINT PETER

Saint Peter was known as the high priest and seal of the martyrs, as he was the final martyr during the reign of Emperor Diocletian. He was born in the third century AD and was martyred in the year 311 AD. He became archbishop from the years 300-311 AD, He wrote many letters and worked wonders during his occupancy as patriarch.

St Peter

Other Names The Seal of Martyrs, 17th Pope of Alexandria

Birth 3rd century AD

Feast Hator 29/ November 8 (departure).

Saint Peter's mother, was of old age and barren, yet she remained fervent and devout in her spiritual life. On the feast day of Saint Peter and Saint Paul, she went to church and was exceedingly sorrowful when she saw all the mothers present with their young children. That night, St Peter and St Paul appeared to her and told her in a vision that the Lord had accepted her prayers and He would give her a son that she would name Peter. They commanded her to go to the Patriarch the next day to bless her. She awoke the next morning over joyed and went to the Patriarch who prayed and blessed her.

Peter was devoted to God from an early age. At the mere age of seven, Peter was presented to the church to be trained in both his studies and scripture. His eagerness to learn and understand the Holy writings resulted in him becoming a lecturer by the age of thirteen and "*knew how to recite in such a way that everyone came early to church because of the sweetness with which he read the lessons.*" It is likely that towards the end of the third century, Peter was the head of the catechetical school in Alexandria where Origen had also directed.

In the year 300 AD, Saint Peter succeeded Pope Theonas as the Patriarch of the see of Alexandria. Theonas himself was instructed by the Lord to appoint Peter to succeed him in his seat as he was told, "*You who water well the spiritual garden, give the garden to Peter the presbyter so he can water it, and come and rest with your fathers.*" These are very beautiful words from God who anointed Saint Peter in the same manner in which He anointed King David the Prophet, highlighting the piety of Saint Peter and the amount of trust that the Lord placed in him.

In the year 303 AD, the nineteenth year of Diocletian's reign over the Roman Empire and the fourth year in which Saint Peter overtook the See of Alexandria, the mass persecutions of Christians began. At the start of the following year, Bishop Peter fled to try to reduce the persecution of the church, and to continue to minister to his beloved church from a secure location. Whilst some may view this as fear, it was in fact in St Peter's abundant wisdom and understanding to flee to someplace where he was still able to serve the church, until the time would come for his martyrdom.

Peter returned from exile in the year 311 AD and his last years as Pope coincided with the appearance of Arius the heretic. Saint Peter advised Arius to get rid of his wicked thoughts, but to no avail. Accordingly, he had no option but to excommunicate him and prevent him from the unity of the church. Arius, in anger, reported Saint Peter to the authorities under Diocletian, saying that he had incited people not to worship idols. The Emperor was outraged and sent messengers to Alexandria with orders to cut off his head.

Upon arrival, the messengers of the Emperor proceeded to kill the Christians, captured the Patriarch and imprisoned him. When his followers were made aware of his imprisonment, there was uproar in front of the prison doors by the Christians who wanted to save him by force. The guard who was assigned to slay him became anxious that the general peace would be disturbed and so he delayed the execution to the following day. When St. Peter saw what had occurred, he wanted to deliver himself to death for his people so that they would not be harmed. He yearned to depart and be with Christ so he sent for his people, comforted them and instructed them to remain in the true faith.

Arius, who was excommunicated at the time, learned that Saint Peter would soon depart to be with Christ, pleaded to him through the high priests to absolve him. Saint Peter refused his request and told them that Jesus had appeared to him in a vision wearing a robe that was torn. When Saint Peter asked Him why His robe was torn, the Lord replied, *"Arius has rent My robe, because he separated Me from My Father. Beware of accepting him."* After passing on this final message, Saint Peter called for the Emperor's officer in secret and ordered him to dig a hole in the prison's wall on the side where no Christians were, so that no one would try to save him. The officer was amazed by his bravery and did as he was asked, taking him to the tomb of St Mark outside to be killed. There, Saint Peter knelt down and asked the Lord that the shedding of his blood would signal the end of the persecution of the Christians. A voice from heaven came saying, *"Amen. May it be according to your wishes,"* and his head was cut off. The people, upon finding out what had occurred, went hurriedly to the place where he was martyred, took his pure body and dressed it in the pontifical clothes to seat him on the seat of St Mark where he refused to sit on during his eleven years as Pope.

St. Peter became for us a man whose life resembled the scriptures, which is fitting for a man who spent his life learning, understanding and living by them. He obtained the crown of martyrdom on the 29th of the Coptic month of Hator 311AD.

SAINT JOHN CHRYSOSTOM

Saint John Chrysostom had incredible influence on the church when Christianity was in turmoil. This earned him the title, "Chrysostom" or "The Golden Mouth." He was also considered a doctor of the church. He spoke fluently and with great sweetness that drew many back to the true faith.

He was born in 347 AD Antioch, Syria. He was the only son of Secundus, a commander of the imperial troops and Anthusa. His father died when his mother was 20 years old, soon after John's birth. She instructed him down the path of piety and valued his education.

Saint John Chrysostom studied law and was not baptised until he was over the age of twenty, as was the custom of the

St John Chrysostom

Other Names The Golden Mouth, Doctor of the Church, Archbishop of Constantinople,

Birth 347 AD

Feast Hator 17/November 26 (departure),

Tout 16/ September 26 (translocation of relics),

Bashans 12/ May 20 (relocation of relics)

Famous Quote "If God had not intended to raise us up again, if it was His desire that we should all be dissolved and blotted out in annihilation, He would not have wrought so many things for us. He would have not spread the heavens above, or stretched out the earth beneath. He would have not fashioned this whole universe, if it were only for the short span of our lives. I beseech you, do not reason, nor be ignorant of the riches God spread out before you. From the beginning, God desired to make you immortal but you were unwilling."

time. Having turned against the teaching of Libanius, he became a monk.

Under the guidance of Diodous, he attended a school for monks. In 374 AD, he joined a community of hermits and resided in the mountains of south Antioch.

For four years, he was guided by a Syrian monk named, "Hesychius," that is to say, "quietness" for four years. Through the virtue of quietness, John wished to expel physical pleasure and the pain he had after his mother's departure. He then moved to a small cave in solitude where he denied himself sleep and would read the Bible continually. For two years, he refused to lie down. This resulted in his stomach shrivelling and his kidneys and digestive tract were impaired.

In 381 AD, he was forced to come down from the mountain due to his physical ailments. Upon his return, he was ordained a priest of Antioch. At age of forty, Bishop Flavian appointed him a preacher and he continued in this service for 12 years. He regarded servitude of the poor as his main priority. He had no greater desire than that the whole of Antioch turn to Christ. At that time, the Christian congregation was about 100 000.

In 387 AD, Bishop Flavian was absent and the people of Antioch were being executed. He encouraged the people through 20 homilies, "On the Statues." He spoke of God's mercy and things that were far worse than death or slavery so that the people would embrace execution with courage for the greatness of the Kingdom that awaited. These homilies were delivered daily and strengthened the Christians and they were filled with hope and joy despite torture and imprisonment. In due time, Saint John Chrysostom was called to glorify God's name upon a new stage.

After the death of Nectarius, Archbishop of Constantinople in 397AD, Saint John Chrysostom was chosen as his successor. He was given a luxurious palace that was situated beside the Emperor's palace. He despised riches and longed for a life of simplicity. He emptied the palace and all costly marble and furnishing and with the profits, he built a hospital for the poor and needy. He reformed the clergy and within three months, they were greatly against his reforms.

After a horse race conducted on Good Friday, Saint John Chrysostom delivered a powerful sermon that condemned the wealth of the people of Constantinople with their marble floors of gold, silver couches and ivory doors. He ridiculed their marriages because they were centred around dancers and singers that accompanied the bride and groom after the marriage ceremony. He objected against mourners at funerals, against slavery and supported the equality of women.

Empress Eudoxia was a supporter of Saint John until he was wrongly accused of calling her "Jezebel." She conspired to depose him in 403AD. As a result, the city of Constantinople was in turmoil for three days. John was exiled but returned soon after an earthquake hit the city. After speaking against a large silver statue of the Empress that was erected before the church, he was deposed again for two months. For the final three years of his life, he endured various exiles and deteriorating health.

In 407 AD, he uttered his final words saying, "Glory be to God for all things," and gave up his holy soul in Commana, Pontus. His departure is commemorated on 17th day of the Coptic month of Hator.

In 438 AD, his body was returned to Constantinople and was received with great joy by Emperor Theodosius II. This is commemorated on the 16th day of the Coptic month of Tout. Later his relics were relocated from Comana to Constantinople. This is commemorated on the 12th day of the Coptic month of Bashans.

SAINT THEODOSIUS

Saint Theodosius was born during the 6th century AD. There was intense theological and social fragmentation during the time Saint Theodosius entered the Patriarchy of the See of Saint Mark in 536 A.D. Theologically, the council of Chalcedon (451 A.D.) had produced a separation of the Copts from the Ecumenical Church, whereby those in opposition to it were labelled "Monophysites" of which the Alexandrian Church was considered the foremost. Socially, this only served to heighten local instability for the Roman Emperor Justinian, who had sided with the the council and had inherited from his Uncle (Justin I) a regime which attempted to thwart any anti-Chalcedonian sentiment. These issues compounded during his thirty year papacy to create a difficult time for Pope Theodosius I.

St Theodosius

Other Names 33rd Patriarch of Alexandria

Birth 6th century AD

Feast Paona 28/June 22 (departure)

Famous Quote "Look! I see the heavens opened and the Son of Man standing at the right hand of God!"

During his time as secretary to Pope Timothy III in 536 AD, Theodosius had grown close to the Antiochian Church Patriarch Pope Severus, who supported Theodosius in his election to papacy. Immediately after being elected as the 33rd Pope of the Coptic Church, an Archdeacon named Gaianus with Julianist supporters sought to forcibly remove the pope. This action uprooted a twenty year Severan-Julianist division, bringing to surface many of the social and theological issues Theodosius would face among the Egyptian people. The revolt, that ensued, forced Theodosius to escape to Constantinople, where he was to remain for only 104 days.

Upon learning of the dethronement of Theodosius, Queen Theodora (who was a Coptic sympathizer), approached Emperor Justinian and asked to have Theodosius re-enthroned as patriarch. Justinian accepted and sent a legion of 6,000 troops, with the Eunuch Narses, to restore order and remove Gaianus. To restore his authority once more Theodosius immediately convenes a local Synod, professing his support to the fathers and councils which preceded him including the writings of St Cyril and the teachings of Nicaea and Ephesus. This served to improve Theodosius' relationship with the exiled Pope Severus, who likened his struggle to that of the Apostle Paul, and Aaron of the Old Testament.

Although Gaianus' reign was short-lived, his revolt was never fully extinguished, leading to violent riots between the Severans and Julianists and resulting in the death of almost 3 000 rioters. After only 17 months, in the Autumn of 536 AD, Theodosius departed for Constantinople to be permanently exiled.

Upon landing in Constantinople, Theodosius was received by Emperor Justinian and Queen Theodora. For one year, the Emperor attempted to force Saint Theodosius to accept the Chalcedonic creed but he continued to defy him which led to the first ever deposition of a Bishop by an Emperor. In his place, Justinian appointed a Chalcedonian monk named Paul Tabenessiota, which further fragmented the Egyptians into three groups. The Emperor went so far as to lock the doors of Coptic Churches for a year before giving the keys to Paul and the Chalcedonians. When Severus passed away in 538 A.D. Theodosius became the ecumenical head of the anti-Chalcedonic movement in Egypt and used this to reunite the Copts. While in exile in Constantinople protected by Queen Theodora inside the Palace of Hormisdas, Theodosius began to proactively engage his diocese by committing himself to three main tasks. He first began by battling heresy through his writings. Theodosius wrote against two main heresies including i) Tritheism (in De Trinitate - 557 A.D.) led by John Ascoutzanges and the ii) Agnoetie movement led by Themistius. Recently discovered primary evidence (2013), including a dossier of 45 letters written by bishops including Theodosius, indicate that his work on the Trinity "is considered the touchstone for orthodoxy," and it served as a major influence in dispelling the tritheistic heresy in the non-Chalcedonian churches. Secondly Theodosius worked on appointing several bishops such as Jacob Baradaeus and several missionaries for Syria and Arabia, re-establishing churches and spreading the Gospel. His third effort included producing homilies such as that of the Dormition and Assumption of the Virgin Mary.

A year after the death of Emperor Justinian, on the succession of his son Emperor Justin II to the throne in 565, St Theodosius was granted permission to return to Alexandria, but he reposed in the Lord before departing.

After his death, he was venerated and was buried in Constantinople with Patriarchal honours.

Despite living through intense difficulty and struggle, Saint Theodosius may be remembered for his ability to stand up confidently for the Coptic church in the face of mounting pressure by the members of the Emperor and Chalcedonic churches. He also defended the Church against the growth of the Tritheist and Agnoetie heresies which threatened to divide the Copts. Theodosius was also well trained and learned in literature and writing and used his talent to provide the notable Homily of the Dormition and Assumption of the Virgin Mary, which until today is well regarded amongst scholars as one of the main secondary sources for Assumption by the Church. Although Theodosius faced "a multi layered schism that wracked the Egyptian church and largely hindered his efforts, he still managed to influence some form of lasting theological change on the Coptic population of his time and for future generations to come. His departure is commemorated on the 28th day of the Coptic month of Paona.

SAINT THEOPHILUS

Saint Theophilus was the 23rd Pope of Alexandria. He was a disciple of the great Saint Athanasius the Apostolic and imitated him in leadership and in spiritual strife. Pope Cyril I was also his nephew and he ensured that his spiritual life was taken care of from a young age, sending him to Abba Serapion in the wilderness of Scetes.

While little is known of his early life, when Pope Timothy I departed, Theophilus was chosen as the next Patriarch. Pope Theophilus displayed knowledge and was well read in the church books with an ability to interpret and decipher meaning. He was mostly well-known for urging his congregation toward acts of charity and mercy.

St Theophilus

Other Names 23rd Patriarch of Alexandria

Birth 5AD

Feast Baba 18/ October 28 (departure)

Mesra 14/ August 20 (the great sign)

Saint Athanasius had a strong desire to build a church for Saint John the Baptist and Elisha the prophet in the hills where he dwelt. Saint Theophilus remembered the words of his teacher and eagerly wanted to fulfil his wish during his own patriarchy. A recently widowed woman from the city of Rome came to Alexandria with great wealth that had been left to her following her husband's departure. She knew of Saint Theophilus' wish and gave him enough money to remove the hills of Scetes and build in their place a church in the name of Saint John the Baptist and Elisha the prophet.

When work was completed and the hills removed, a treasure was revealed with three Coptic letters of theta. Upon seeing this, Saint Theophilus marvelled and said, *"Behold the time has come for this treasure to be uncovered because these three thetas were gathered together at the same time and they are: Thoes, that of God; and Theodosius the Emperor, son of Arcadius, son of Theodosius the Great; and Theophilus the Patriarch."*

Saint Theophilus informed the Emperor of the great treasure that had been found. He immediately came and saw the discovery. He gave a large sum of money to Pope Theophilius that was more than enough to build several churches in the area. The first was of course, for Saint John the Baptist and Elisha the Prophet where their relics were transferred. The second was in the name of Saint Mary, another in the name of Archangel Raphael and seven other churches followed.

During his papacy, there were two poor Christian men who looked upon a rich Jewish man named Philexinos and desired to possess his wealth. They blasphemed against Christ and thought that their worship of Christ was worth nothing while they remained poor. They asked Philexinos to make them his servants. Philexinos demanded that they deny their Christ and become Jews before he took them in as his servants. He took them to the synagogue where the chief of Jews made them deny their Christ before all the people of the synagogue.

They brought before them a wooden cross and a reed with a sponge filled with vinegar on top. They commanded the two Christian men to spit on the cross and offer vinegar and say with a spear in their hands, "I pierce you O Christ." As they pierced the Cross, blood and water poured forth and fell to the ground. The two former Christian men instantly died and their bodies dried up. Many were converted to Christianity at this sight. Pope Theophilus was called to the scene. He, along with Bishops and priests, went and blessed themselves with the blood and water that flowed from the Cross. As for Philexinos, he anointed the eyes of his daughter who was born blind, she immediately received sight. Pope Theophilus baptised him and many Jews in the name of the Father, the Son and the Holy Spirit. This miracle is commemorated on the 14th day of the Coptic month of Mesra.

The two sons of the woman who made the initial donation were made bishops. Seeing Pope Theophilus' love for building churches, the Emperor gave him all the houses of idols. He made them churches and lodging houses for the homeless. After 18 years as Patriarch, Pope Theophilus departed in the year 412 AD. Saint Theophilus' departure is commemorated on the 18th day of Baba.

SAINT DEMETRIUS

Saint Demetrius was born in 119 AD to Christian parents. During his early years, Saint Demetrius was forced by his parents to marry. He and his wife lived in virginity for forty-seven years. A fact that was unknown to the people. He was a simple vinedresser of Alexandria and was said to be illiterate.

Pope Julian, 11th Pope of Alexandria, had a vision of an angel who said to him, "*He who comes to you in the morning bringing a bunch of grapes will be your successor.*"

The next morning, Saint Demetrius was harvesting the vineyard and found a cluster of grapes that had ripened before their time. He decided to offer his first fruits to Pope Julian. As soon as Pope Julian

St Demetrius

Other Names Pope Demetrius I, 12th Patriarch of the See of St Mark, The Vinedresser, the fighter of lust and vanquisher of nature.

Birth 119 AD

Feast Baba 12/October 22 (departure)
Baramhat 12/ March 21 (revelation of virginity)

Famous Quote "Turn away from your sin and repent, after that come and partake of the Holy Mysteries."

saw this, he gathered the bishops together and told them that Demetrius would be his successor.

And so it was, after Pope Julian's departure in 191 AD, Demetrius was ordained 12th Pope of Alexandria and the See of Saint Mark. The Lord enlightened his heart and mind so he learnt to read and write even the most theological texts. It is said of Pope Demetrius that words of grace flew from his mouth when he spoke.

During his papacy, he established the epacts – that is, the number of days – for fasting periods. Prior to Saint Demetrius, the Christians fasted 40 days of Lent immediately following the Epiphany and Holy Week was fasted separately, later in the year. The Christian Passover was the Sunday that followed the Jewish Passover. Some Christians held April 14 as the day of Passover and would sometimes celebrate Passover with the Jews. In this way, there was no recognition of the Resurrection of the Lord Jesus Christ.

It was for this reason that Pope Demetrius established a fixed period of fasting and the holy days. He invented a special calendar that combined solar and lunar years and adjusted the feast of the Resurrection so that it would not come before the 1st of April and not after the 1st of May. This was then accepted by the holy Senate in Alexandria. A century later, the fathers of the Council of Nicea adopted Saint Demetrius' calendar among the Catholic church as well. The Catholic church upheld this tradition until 1582 AD. Beyond this point, they began to celebrate the Resurrection the first Sunday after the full moon, irrespective of any clashes with the Jewish Passover.

God gave Saint Demetrius many spiritual gifts, including the ability to recognise if someone was prepared to receive the divine sacraments during Holy Communion. When distributing the divine Mystery, he would see the Hand of the Lord Christ pushing forward those who were worthy and pushing back those who were not. For those that were unworthy, their sins were revealed to Pope Demetrius who would deny them Communion until they had repented and confessed their sins.

There was rebuke among non-repentant sinners who questioned the legitimacy of his judgement. He was, after all, a married man and there was false assumptions made of his virginity. During that time, monasticism had not yet been established but there had not been a married Patriarch till Pope Demetrius I.

The Lord wished to reveal to the people the purity of Abba Demetrius and so the angel of the Lord came to him by night and said,

"Demetrius, do not seek your salvation and let others be destroyed with their doubt. You must reveal the mystery which is between yourself and your wife to the people that you might remove doubt from them. You are their Shepherd, you should fight to save them from ill-thoughts."

After praying the liturgy on the next day, Pope Demetrius asked the people not to leave the church. He brought flamed charcoal before the people. He prayed then walked upon the blazing fire. Taking a piece of flaming charcoal, he placed it in his shawl and took another piece and placed it in his wife's shawl. Praying again, neither one of the shawls was set on fire. The people were amazed and implored him to tell them why neither of them was burnt by the fire.

Saint Demetrius explained to the people the spiritual strife he and his wife had chosen, by living in celibacy. They had been living as brother and sister since their parents forced them to marry forty-eight years earlier. The angel of the Lord would cover them with their wings and no one knew the extent of their purity until the angel ordered him to reveal their secret to them.

The people marvelled and begged for his forgiveness of their prior condemnation and judgement of their marriage. He forgave and blessed them so that they would give glory to God. The revelation of the virginity of Pope Demetrius and his wife is commemorated on the 12th day of the Coptic month of Baramhat.

In 194 AD, he endured a period of exile under the persecution of Septimius Severus. During this time, Saint Liondias, father of Origen, was exiled, Origen was appointed dean of the catechumen's School of Alexandria. A heresy of the death of the human spirit began to spread, Origen was sent to teach the Christians the way of Orthodoxy. He established a catechumen school in Asia Minor and accepted the ordination of priesthood from the Bishop of Jerusalem and the Bishop of Caesarea of Cappadocia. It is believed that Pope Demetrius responded by exiling Origen for accepting ordination from a pope that was not his own. This was not an official rule at that time and so, it was possible that Origen remained in Jerusalem on his own accord, and even had the blessing of Pope Demetrius.

After 43 years as Patriarch, at the age of 105, Pope Demetrius departed in peace in the year 224AD. His departure is commemorated on the 12th day of the Coptic month of Baba.

SAINT CYRIL

Saint Cyril was the 24th Patriarch of the See of Saint Mark. He was a defender of the faith and lamp of the Orthodox church. The liturgy of St Cyril is still prayed in the Coptic Orthodox church till this day.

Saint Cyril was born in 376 AD to Christian parents. His mum was the sister of Pope Theophilius (23rd Pope of Alexandria). He was educated in theology and philosophy at a young age and was mentored by his uncle, Pope Theophilius.

St Cyril

Other Names Pillar of faith, lamp of the Orthodox church, St Cyril I, 24th Pope of Alexandria

Birth 376 AD

Feast Abib 3/June 27 (departure)

Famous Quote "As two pieces of wax fused together make one, so he who receives Holy Communion is so united with Christ is in him and he is in Christ."

After completing his studies, he went to the monastery of Saint Macarius in the wilderness. He was guided by an older monk named Sarabamon who taught him the church books and sayings of the fathers. He became disciplined in works of righteousness and virtues for a long period of time.

After spending five years in the wilderness, Pope Theophilius sent him to Abba Sarapion to increase his knowledge. Abba Sarapion soon returned him to his uncle in Alexandria. Pope Theophilius rejoiced and ordained him a deacon, preacher and his own personal scribe. St Cyril was skilled in giving sermons and captured the hearts of many. He became known for the depth of his knowledge, righteousness and influence.

In 403 AD he went with his uncle to the Synod of the Oak in Constantinople where Saint John Chrysostom was deposed under false accusations. A year prior, Pope Theophilius was also forced to apologise before a synod for false accusations raised by Egyptian monks.

When his uncle departed in the year 412 AD, Cyril was quickly elected as the next Patriarch of Alexandria. Despite the tension of heresy that were still looming, Pope Cyril proved to be knowledgeable and concise in his approach to preaching. Emperor Julian had composed 10 essays that were believed by the people of Alexandria to refute the Christian faith. Pope Cyril was clear, strong and convincing in disproving Emperor Julian's heresy.

In 428 AD, the heresy of Nestorius caused a lot of division in the church. Nestorius believed that St Mary was rightfully the, "*mother of Christ*" and not the "*mother of God*." Two hundred bishops assembled at Ephesus in what was to become the third Ecumenical Council in 431 AD. Saint Cyril debated with Nestorius and threatened him with excommunication if he did not change his ways. St Cyril composed 12 discourses that explained the true faith and refuted Nestorius' beliefs.

John of Antioch and other pro-Nestorius bishops of the east reached Ephesus and assembled their own Council that condemned St Cyril for heresy and deposed him. The Emperor ordered Saint Cyril's arrest but he eventually escaped and fled to Egypt. The bishops of the east eventually realised the error of their ways and Nestorius was exiled in 435 AD.

St Cyril departed in 440 AD, having spent 31 years as Pope of Alexandria. His departure is commemorated on the 3rd day of the Coptic month of Abib.

Saint Basil the Great

Saint Basil was born in the year 330 AD in Cappadocia. He was born to a pious family, many of whom are also saints. These include his grandmother Saint Macrina along with his brother Saint Gregory of Nyssa.

Saint Basil, Saint Gregory of Nyssa and their friend Saint Gregory of Nazianzus (also known as Saint Gregory the Theologian) are collectively referred to as the Cappadocian Fathers and contributed greatly to the commentaries on Scripture that are read till this day. Saint Basil's life emulated the verse, *"Do not be deceived: "Evil company corrupts good habits"* - 1 Cor. 15:35. If ever there was an example that the converse of this is true, it is there in Saint Basil who was surrounded by saints.

Saint Basil was a true academic person and he spent time as a young adult learning at the feet of scholars in Constantinople and Athens. It was in Athens

St Basil the Great

Other Names St Basil the Great, St Basil the Theologian

Birth 330 AD

Feast Toba 6/January 14 (departure)

Famous Quote "We must try to keep in mind tranquillity. For just as the eye which constantly shifts its gaze, now turning to the right or to the left, now incessantly peering up and down, cannot see distinctly what lies before it, but the sight must be fixed firmly on the object in view if one would make his vision of it clear, so too man's mind when distracted by his countless worldly cares cannot focus itself distinctly on the truth."

where he met his great friend Saint Gregory of Nazianzus. He advanced in knowledge, virtue and asceticism, which led him to visit many monastic communities in Egypt, Palestine and Syria. He was influenced by the great Saint Pachomious during his time in the Egyptian Desert.

Bishop Eusebius in Cappadocia ordained him a priest at the age of 35, a natural consequence of Saint Basil's immersion in theology and asceticism. Unfortunately, Saint Basil's popularity led to some discord within the clergy. Saint Gregory of Nazianzus relates *"But seeing that everyone exceedingly praised and honoured Basil for his wisdom and reverence, Eusebius, through human weakness, succumbed to jealousy of him, and began to show dislike for him."* The monks rose up in defence of Saint Basil. To avoid causing Church discord, Saint Basil withdrew to his own monastery and concerned himself with the organization of monasteries.

With the coming to power of the emperor Valens (364-378 AD), who was a resolute adherent of Arianism, a time of trouble began for the church. Saint Basil hastily returned to Caesarea at the request of Bishop Eusebius. Saint Gregory, speaking about the activity of Basil the Great during this period, points to *"the caring for the destitute and the taking in of strangers, the supervision of virgins, the written and unwritten monastic rules for monks, the arrangement of prayers* [Liturgy].*"* Upon the death of Eusebius, the Bishop of Caesarea, Saint Basil was chosen to succeed him in the year 370 AD. Unfortunately, the turmoil continued during Saint Basil's time as bishop, primarily by the impious emperor Valens, who tried to impose Arianism on the region.

Valens would mercilessly send into exile any bishop who displeased him, and having implanted Arianism into other Asia Minor provinces, this suddenly appeared in Saint Basil's Cappadocia for this same purpose. He began to threaten the saint with the confiscation of his property, banishment, beatings, and even death. As expected, this did not seem to bother Saint Basil at all. What was surprising however, was the boldness with which Saint Basil expressed his disdain for such threats. St Basil replied to Valens,

"If you take away my possessions, you will not enrich yourself, nor will you make me a pauper. You have no need of my old worn-out clothing, nor of my few books, of which the entirety of my wealth is comprised. Exile means nothing to me, since I am bound to no particular place. This place in which I now dwell is not mine, and any place you send me shall be mine… Who can torture me? I am so weak, that the very first blow would render me insensible. Death would be a kindness to me, for it will bring me all the sooner to God, for Whom I live and labour, and to Whom I hasten."

Emperor Valens was stunned by his answer. *"No one has ever spoken so audaciously to me,"* he said. *"Perhaps,"* the saint remarked, *"that is because you've never spoken to a bishop before!"* Saint Basil was a man of humility, meekness and prayer. However when the circumstance and the service of God required it, he spoke with great boldness and power.

It is perhaps for his theology and writings that Saint Basil is mostly remembered for. He was side by side with Saint Athanasius, defending the divinity of Christ against the Arians at the first Ecumenical Council in Nicea. He also wrote his treatise "On the Holy Spirit" defending the divinity of the Holy Spirit, which thankfully has been published and translated to English. Along with his great friend Saint Gregory of Nazianzus, they studied the scriptures deeply, relying on the wisdom of their predecessors particularly Origen the Scholar. Together they wrote the Philokalia, a great source of wisdom and a book considered by many to be second only to the Holy Bible. Saint Basil is of course responsible for the liturgy that is prayed most often in Coptic Orthodox Churches today.

Sickly since youth, the toil of teaching, his life of abstinence, and the concerns and sorrows of pastoral service took their toll on him. St Basil died on January 14, 379 AD at age 49. His departure is commemorated on 6th day of the Coptic month of Toba.

SAINT GREGORY THE THEOLOGIAN

Saint Gregory was the middle child of Saint Gregory the Elder and Saint Nonna, and was born around 330 AD. His father was from a pagan background, however through the prayers of Saint Nonna (who Gregory consistently presented as his spiritual powerhouse), he was converted to Christianity and even became the Bishop of Nazianzus. His younger brother Ceasarios became a physician and a saint. In fact, the whole of Saint Gregory's immediate family are saints in the Eastern Orthodox Church.

As was the custom in those days, when boys were matured in age, they began an educational tour of the eastern world. Throughout his travels, the main intellectual dilemma faced by Christians everywhere was the practical effect of the Nicene Creed,

St Gregory the Theologian

Other Names Gregory Nazianzus, the brother of Saint Basil the Great

Birth 330 AD

Feast Toba 21/ October 1 (departure)

Famous Quote "'As a fish cannot swim without water, and as a bird cannot fly without air, so a Christian cannot advance a single step without Christ.' Not to every one, my friends, does it belong to philosophize about God; not to every one; the Subject is not so cheap and low; and I will add, not before every audience, nor at all times, nor on all points; but on certain occasions, and before certain persons, and within certain limits."

and what this meant for Arianism. It was amidst all these theological arguments and controversy, that Gregory was sharpening his skills. He was already proving to be a very skilled orator, and he immersed himself in reading all the Greek classics. But we find at this point, as was common in the early Church, Gregory was still not baptised.

Gregory made his way through to Alexandria where he encountered Saint Athanasius. In fact, Gregory treated Athanasius as though he were a personal hero. For Gregory, Athanasius represented the true Nicene Faith, and he consistently positioned himself as Athanasius' true successor when it came to leading the Nicene movement.

From there Gregory moved to Athens, which was perhaps one of the most formative times in his life. He made his way from Alexandria to Athens by boat. It was on this boat that Gregory was well and truly converted. There was a storm on the ship that lasted 28 days. Gregory spent the entire time huddled up, petrified, and prayed that he would not depart since he had not been baptised yet. Gregory, was by all accounts, terrified and he states that even after everyone had calmed down, he was still hysterical and crying out to God. Amid this terrifying storm, Gregory made a promise that changed the whole course of his life. He promised to dedicate his life to God. He promised God, that his greatest worldly loves that were rhetoric and cultural learning, he would relinquish to serve God.

Gregory's time in Athens was an incredibly rich time. He met some of the most intelligent minds of his day.

He also became acquainted with Julian, the future Apostate who was to become Emperor. Even during his stay in Athens, Julian was dabbling in the occult, and his confusion is a future source of humour for Gregory when he caricatured him.

For Gregory, Athens was synonymous with Basil. His learning was certainly vast, and he surrounded himself with a group of young ascetics. Together they discussed philosophy and encouraged each other in spiritual endeavours. Their friendship became an example of how the people one surrounds themselves with influence the person one becomes. Gregory and Basil were incredibly close. The first hurt that Gregory experienced was when Basil decided to leave Athens. Basil saw Athens as a stepping stone whereas Gregory could have remained content in Athens for long years to come. Basil longed for a tour of the famous Egyptian ascetical sites, where he could learn from the vast and rich experience of the desert fathers. Basil clearly wanted his freedom and for Gregory this was a hurt that was not healed for 26 years. Gregory saw it as a betrayal and he felt forsaken. The light had gone out of Athens at Basil's departure.

Gregory argues that he was called back home to support his ageing parents (hardly the case if one considers what the man Saint Gregory the Elder was), but it was clear that the reason was that the real heart and soul of Athens, Basil, had left. Gregory stole away during the night and returned to Nazianzus.

Gregory's idea of monasticism was much different to the idea that we have become accustomed to. For Gregory, it was about living in seclusion, practising moderate asceticism and dedicating his life to intellectual endeavours. Basil did not agree with this. He encouraged Gregory to join in in more serious ascetical endeavours, but Gregory was unwilling. For Gregory, it was more about simplicity of lifestyle, rather than physically demanding asceticism. This was not a life that Gregory the Elder considered appropriate for someone like Gregory. If Gregory was not to become a professional orator, then he would have to become priest. This was not something that Gregory had in mind.

Amidst all this, the political context was becoming more and more alarming for Niceans. Julian was declared Emperor in about 360 AD. Julian, though a pagan, had begun to show favour to the Arian party, and brought back many Bishops from exile, even though this often meant two rival bishops in one See. In 361 AD, Gregory's peaceful life was shattered by his father's insistence that Gregory join the Priesthood. Gregory reacted hysterically. He knew that becoming a priest would almost certainly destroy his aspirations for monastic seclusion. However, Gregory's over-bearing father eventually convinced him. On Christmas of 361 AD, Gregory was ordained a Priest. Within a few days, he escaped (as he often did throughout his life) to Basil's monastic retreat. He stayed there for about two months.

A few years later, however, family disaster began to come crashing down on Gregory. In 368 AD, his brother Ceaserios died causing Gregory an unbelievable amount of grief. About a year later, his sister Gorgonia also died. St Gregory went on to become the Bishop of a town called Sasima in the year 372 AD.

The Nicenes realised that they needed to establish a stronger presence in the Capital of Constantinople. It is said that Basil, on his death bed, recommended Gregory to be that presence in the capital, a signal that the old hostility had worn away in the later years. When Gregory entered the capital, it was predominantly Arian. Gregory was forced to turn his lodgings into a church, the Anastasia. Gregory entered the capital in 379 AD. His teaching in the capital changed the whole course of church history, and our understanding of who God is. His contribution in these respects is unbelievable. Once again, Gregory began his mission by stating the true characteristics of a theologian, which is not simply extensive knowledge, but a meaningful relationship with God.

Gregory endured systematic attacks from the Arian party in the city, under the Bishop Demophilos. A crowd of monks and nuns from the city with a bunch of troublemakers destroyed an Easter Vigil service. He was almost assassinated but his assassin could not go through with it. It was during this time at the capital, in 380 AD, that he delivered a series of five orations that earned him the title, 'The Theologian' and forever changed the face of Trinitarian theology. These were orations that established Gregory as the foremost Trinitarian theologian of his day. When he finished these orations, he decided to set off for a retreat. However, during his time in Constantinople, he had made a close friend and ally, Maximus the Cynic. Maximus was sent by the Egyptian Archbishop as an ally to Gregory. Peter of Alexandria became increasingly frustrated with Gregory's reluctance to take the reins of Constantinople and become Archbishop. Therefore, Peter and Maximus decided that Maximus would make a bid for the See, considering Gregory was so hesitant to accept it.

Gregory used a favourite oratorical tactic of threatening resignation to get everyone on his side. It had worked in the past. This time however, it did not work. Gregory lost face completely with the Antiochians. However, Gregory's main problem with the Council was how it was progressing theologically. 36 bishops were present who were Pneumatomachians (Spirit Fighters). Gregory could not compromise on the issue of the divinity of the Spirit. The Council pushed for a theological vagueness in relation to the divinity of the Spirit. Gregory was beginning to feel that the whole council was becoming a pollution of the true faith. Gregory, becoming ill, withdrew from the following sessions of the Council.

What emerged from the Council was the statement about the Holy Spirit that we say in the Creed. If you listen carefully, it has all the vagueness that Gregory hated. The only reason that the Creed is acceptable, is because the interpretation given to it through the writings of Gregory.

Gregory spent the last years of his life in the way that he had always wanted: peaceful ascetic solitude. He wrote many memoirs and poems and delivered a funeral oration for Basil which showed the depth of their love and bond that endured even the many years of hostility. He departed in the year 396 AD and his departure is commemorated on the 21st day of the Coptic month of Toba.

Gregory (originally Theodore, meaning "Gift of God") was born to a pagan family in Neo-Caesarea (capital of Pontus in Asia Minor) in 213 AD. When Theodore was 14, his father died. From this point, Theodore and his brothers were eager to learn, so they studied at the Berytus (Beirut) which was central to the study of Roman Law. Their brother-in-law was assessor (legal counsel) to the Roman Governor of Palestine during the time. Theodore and his brothers had to escort their sister to him in Caesarea in Palestine. Little did they know that this would change their lives forever. When they finally arrived in Caesarea, they heard of a scholar who was extremely reputable, celebrated and brilliant. This scholar was Origen.

Theodore and his brother were greatly inclined from this great theologian and teacher. Over time, their desire

St Gregory the Wonderworker

Other Names Saint Gregory of Neocaesarea

Birth 213 AD

Feast Hator 21/ November 30 (departure)

Famous Quote There is a perfect Trinity, in glory and eternity and sovereignty, neither divided nor estranged. Wherefore there is nothing either created or in servitude in the Trinity; nor anything superinduced, as if at some former period it was non-existent, and at some later period it was introduced. And thus neither was the Son ever wanting to the Father, nor the Spirit to the Son; but without variation and without change, the same Trinity abides forever."

to study Roman Law vanished and they decided to learn from Origen instead. In 239 AD, they converted to Christianity. Gregory describes the method adopted by Origen saying, "*how he mingled a persuasive candour with outbursts of temper and theological argument put cleverly at once and unexpectedly. Persuasive skill rather than bare reasoning, and evident sincerity and an ardent conviction were the means Origen used to make converts.*"

Gregory initially studied philosophy, then theology, but he was always deeply fascinated by philosophy. Gregory's aim was to show that Christianity was in fact the only true and good philosophy! This is admirable since philosophy is used by many non-believers to justify their non-belief.

Having returned to Caesarea, the saint fled from the worldly affairs into which influential townsmen persistently sought to push him. He went into the desert, and attained high spiritual accomplishments through the gifts of clairvoyance and prophecy through fasting and prayer. Saint Gregory loved life in the wilderness and wanted to remain in solitude until the end of his days, but the Lord willed otherwise and he was ordained the bishop of Caesarea in 244 AD.

He was renowned for his miracles, healings, fervent prayer and theological teachings. Gregory was once conversing with philosophers and teachers, when suddenly a harlot came to him and demanded that he pay her money which he owed her for his apparent sinful relations with her. Gregory denied her claims and suggested that she mistook him for another man. She insisted even more and he in turn, gave her the money she requested. As she took the money, she dropped and went into a demonic fit. Gregory then prayed for her and the demons left her.

On one occasion, there were two brothers who were quarrelling over their deceased father's property. They both wanted the lake of his father to themselves. Each brother then gathered their own friends to brawl for the lake. Saint Gregory, hearing this, convinced them to delay the brawl till the next day, and stayed up praying till sunrise. When everyone had come to meet at the lake, it was dried up with only a stream of water creating a boundary so that both brothers had their own share.

Sabellius and Paul of Samosata began a heresy regarding the Holy Spirit which began to spread. Gregory was persistent in his prayers to God through the intercessions of Saint Mary for the truth to be revealed. Saint Mary then appeared to him with John the Theologian wearing arch episcopal vestments. The Virgin commanded that Saint John teach and confess the mystery of the Holy Trinity.

When a persecution against Christians began under the Emperor Decius (249-251 AD), Saint Gregory led his flock to a faraway mountain. A certain pagan, knowing about the hiding place of the Christians, informed the persecutors. Soldiers surrounded the mountain. The saint went out into an open place, raised up his hands to heaven and ordered his deacon to do the same. The soldiers searched the whole mountain and passed by those who were praying several times but they could not see them. They eventually gave up and went back to the city.

In the city they reported that there was nowhere to hide on the mountain; no one was there, and only two trees stood beside each other. The informer was struck with amazement; he repented of his ways and became a fervent Christian. Saint Gregory returned to Caesarea after the end of the persecution. By his blessing church Feasts were established in honour of the martyrs who had suffered for Christ.

By his saintly life, his effective preaching, working of miracles and grace guiding of his flock, the saint steadily increased the number of converts to Christ. When Saint Gregory first ascended his chair, there were only seventeen Christians in Caesarea. At his death, only seventeen pagans remained in the city.

Saint Gregory the Wonderworker departed in peace in the year 270 AD. His departure is commemorated on the 21st day of the Coptic month of Hator.

SAINT GREGORY THE ARMENIAN

Saint Gregory was the Patriarch of the Armenians and lived as a confessor and defender of the faith. Although he did not die a martyr, he was persecuted severely by the Tiridates.

Gregory was born in 257 AD to Armenian Parthian nobles. While his parents were not Christian, they gave him to Phirmilianos (Euthalius) to learn Christian teachings. He became devout and knowledgeable.

St Gregory the Armenian

Other Names The Illuminator

Birth 257 AD

Feast Kiahk 15/ December 24 (departure)
Tout 19/ September 29 (commemoration)

In the year 272 AD, a decree was ordered to worship idols. Saint Gregory refused and disobeyed the king. As a result, the king of Armenia cast Saint Gregory into an empty pit where he dwelled for 15 years. During this time, God sustained him. An old widow lived near the pit and she saw a vision of someone telling her to make bread regularly and throw it into the pit. She would do this every day for the 15 years - unknown to her – that Saint Gregory was in the pit. No one knew if Saint Gregory was even alive or not after he was thrown into the pit.

The king endured much affliction for his torture of the Christians. Most notably, he killed Arbisma and all the virgins with her. This pained him deeply for previously, he wished to marry her. His family saw the pain he was in and advised him to go to the mountains, hunt and kill to recreate himself.

While he was riding, the devil took hold of him and dragged him to the ground. King Tridates was possessed with a wild spirit that took the form of a wild boar. The people of the kingdom were afraid to approach him. Many others became possessed in a similar fashion. Great fear took hold over the people of the kingdom.

The sister of the king was plagued with the same vision three nights in a row. She saw a man telling her to bring Saint Gregory out of the pit. If she didn't, her brother, the king would not be cured. This came as a great shock to the people for they believed he had been dead for 15 years. They went to the pit, dropped a rope and called out to him. Gregory moved the rope, giving them the signal that he was still alive.

Gregory was taken to the palace with the people who begged him to cure the king. He made him promise not to turn back to his evil ways. The king agreed and Gregory prayed over him, and the evil spirit departed. While his mind and soul were returned to normal, his nails remained in the likeness of a boar as a constant reminder so he would not return to his former ways. This miracle is commemorated on the 19th day of the Coptic month of Tout.

Later, Gregory asked about the place of burial of Arbisma and the virgins. He found their bodied decayed and he moved them to an honourable location. Saint Gregory the Armenian is known for his ability to cure the sick and cast out demons. Many churches were built, bishops and priests were ordained during the Patriarchy of Gregory. His departure is commemorated on the 15th of the Coptic month of Kiahk.

PART 3
DEFENDERS OF THE FAITH

THE 318 ASSEMBLED AT NICAEA

The Council of Nicea, in the year 325AD, was a critical event in the history of the church, where 318 fathers defeated the heresy of Arius, who argued that the Son was not equal to the Father. Among the defenders of the faith were St. Alexander, the 19th Pope of Alexandria, and St. Athanasius the Apostolic, who was a deacon at that time and would go on to become the 20th Pope of Alexandria.

Arius (from whom the term "Arianism" is derived) was a member of the clergy in Alexandria who had begun propagating that Christ was not eternal, but rather, there was a time when the Son did not exist. He also expressed that the Son was not of the same essence as the Father. He was an eloquent speaker, and would spread his heresies subtly, and even insert them into popular songs. He is famed for the heretical phrase "there was a time when the Son was not."

318 at Nicaea

Feast November 18/Hatour 9

Famous Quote "And those" who say "there once was when he was not", and "before he was begotten he was not", and that he came to be from things that were not, or from another hypostasis or substance, affirming that the Son of God is subject to change or alteration - these the catholic and apostolic church anathematises."

This created significant dispute, and so the council of Nicea (in modern day Turkey) was convened by the

Emperor Constantine and is recognised as the First Ecumenical Council. In attendance were 318 bishops, and Socrates Scholasticus, a historian, who was born in the 4th century, is recorded as describing: "*... in this assembly the number of bishops exceeded three hundred; while the number of presbyters, deacons, and acolyths and others who attended them was almost incalculable.*"

Many of the fathers had been previously persecuted for their love for Christ. Theodoret of Cyrus, a fourth century author, remarks that: *"many, like the holy apostle, bore in their bodies the marks of the Lord Jesus Christ...Paul, Bishop of Neo-Caesarea, a fortress situated on the banks of the Euphrates, had suffered from the frantic rage of Licinius (once a colleague of Emperor Constantine). He had been deprived of the use of both hands by the application of red-hot iron, by which the nerves which give motion to the muscles had been contracted and rendered dead. Some had the right eye dug out, others had lost the right arm. Among these was Paphnutius of Egypt. In short the Council looked like an assembled army of martyrs."*

By the grace of God, the heresy was defeated, and the fathers of the Council of Nicea confessed the Orthodox faith. They produced for us the Nicene Creed, professing our faith. We still proclaim this creed today (with further additions from later council).

An English version of the professions of the Nicene Council, before any additions or omissions were completed at Constantinople, included the following words:

We believe "in one God the Father all powerful, maker of all things both seen and unseen. And in one Lord Jesus Christ, the Son of God, the only-begotten from the Father, that is from the substance of the Father, God from God, light from light, true God from true God, begotten not made, consubstantial with the Father, through whom all things came to be, both those in heaven and those on Earth; for us humans and for our salvation he came down and became incarnate, became human, suffered and rose up on the third day, went up into the heavens, and is coming to judge the living and the dead. And in the Holy Spirit.

And those who say, "there once was when he was not", and "before he was begotten he was not", and that he came to be from things that were not, or from another hypostasis or substance, affirming that the Son of God is subject to change or alteration - these the catholic and apostolic church anathematizes.

Other happenings at Nicea, apart from addressing Arianism, included, working towards setting a date for Easter, attending to the Meletian Schism, and considering certain Christians who had renounced the faith during a time of persecution and wanted to be accepted again.

Another outcome of the council of Nicea was 20 canons or rules, which addressed several topics that purposed to influence the lives of the clergy and the wider church community. The 318 at Nicea are commemorated on the 9th day of the Coptic month of Hator.

The One Hundred and Fifty at Constantinople

The One Hundred and Fifty at Constantinople refers to the one hundred and fifty bishops that responded to Emperor Theodosius' call for a second Ecumenical Council to convene in Constantinople in 381AD.

One Hundred and Fifty at Constantinople

Feast February 17

Famous Quote "Yes, we believe in the Holy Spirit, the Lord, the Life-Giver, who proceeds from the Father."

The Council of Constantinople was deemed necessary after a heresy that denied the Holy Spirit as divine was proclaimed by Macedonius, bishop of Constantinople.

At that time, Abba Timotheus was ordained 22nd successor of the See of St Mark, Pope Timotheus was a disciple of St Athanasius and firm teacher of the Apostolic faith.

When word reached of the heresy that was being spread by Macedonius, the orthodox bishops and trustees of the apostolic legacy believed that another Ecumenical council was essential. Emperor Theodosius agreed and invited the bishops to convene in Constantinople for the matter to be heard.

The Councils aimed to address the following:

The Macedonian Heresy

It was unanimously decided that the Macedonian heresy be overruled; the Holy Spirit was divine. As a result, the Creed was modified to ensure that this was explicitly stated. The Orthodox Creed was, as a result, expanded to include the following affirmation of the Holy Spirit and the oneness of the church;

Yes, we believe in the Holy Spirit, the Lord, the Life-Giver, who proceeds from the Father. Who, with the Father and the Son, is worshipped and glorified, who spoke in the prophets. And in one holy, Catholic (Universal) and Apostolic Church. We confess one baptism for the remission of sins. We look for the resurrection of the dead, and the life of the coming age. Amen.

The Heresy of Apollinarius

The council also discussed the heresy of Apollinarius that preached Jesus Christ as fully divine, but did not believe in His human nature. He believed that Christ did not require a soul because God, the Father, provided for all His needs. This idea was rejected by the Council of Constantinople on the basis that Christ was fully divine but also fully human.

Transfer of diocese

Another issue that was addressed at the Council of Constantinople was the re-affirmation that a bishop remains in the See he was ordained to. A bishop was not to leave his diocese for another unless under exceptional circumstances. This decision had to be agreed upon by numerous bishops in order to be allowed.

At the end of the Council, Timotheus returned to Alexandria. There were many peaceful years while Emperor Theodosius reigned with many churches built and the return of many Arians to the faith.

PART 4
Inhabitants of Scetes

Saint Anthony the Great

Saint Anthony the Great was a third century anchorite, who became known as the father of monasticism. Saint Anthony was born in Helakroplais, Magna in 251AD to Christian parents who possessed considerable wealth. From a young age, he would often separate himself from the activities of children and instead attend church, keeping in his heart what was profitable in what he heard.

At the age of eighteen, the death of his parents left him orphaned with the responsibility to care for both his home and his sister. Saint Anthony's calling began one day as he was walking to church and he began pondering on how the Apostles gave up everything they had to follow our Saviour (Matt 4:20. He thought of the early church congregation recorded in Acts who sold their possessions and brought them to the feet of the apostles to be distributed to the poor and needy. Great hope was laid before them and Saint Anthony wanted to be similar.

St Anthony the Great

Other Names The Father of Monasticism

Birth 251 AD

Feast January 30/ Toba 22 (departure)

Famous quote "If we would despise the enemy, our thoughts must always be of God and our souls always glad with hope"

He entered the church that day to receive the words of the gospel, which read *"if you want to be perfect, go sell what you have and give to the poor, and you will have treasure in heaven; and come follow Me"*, (Matt 19:21). Having heard these words Anthony received the message personally and immediately gave away the three hundred acres of fertile land that he had inherited. The rest of his possessions he sold and distributed the money to the poor keeping back a little for his sister.

It happened again that when Anthony went to church he heard the Lord saying in the gospel, *"Therefore do not worry about tomorrow, for tomorrow will worry about its own things"* (Matt 6:34). This compelled him to leave all his possessions and reside in the desert. He entrusted his sister to a known and faithful house of virgins and gave away all his remaining possessions. Anthony then began to practise ascetic disciplines outside his house in the villages.

When he heard of a certain man who lived as a hermit from his youth he also imitated him in virtue and began to abide in places outside the villages. Whenever Anthony heard of a good man, he would seek him, learn from him his virtues and was obedient to all those who devoted themselves to ascetic disciplines.

Anthony continued to learn many disciplines and virtues from those living in ascetism, and so Satan instigated many attacks on him. Satan first tried to lead him away from the ascetic discipline by whispering to him the remembrance of his wealth, care for his sister, love for money, glory and the difficulty and labour of living virtuously. Anthony was disturbed at night and harassed by day. The devil whispered impure thoughts and by night took the shape of a woman and imitated her acts simply to beguile Anthony. But Anthony's mind being filled with Christ and the spiritual insight quenched the coal of the Devil's deceit.

As Anthony's zeal for asceticism increased, he set out alone to the outer mountain where he lived in a cave. Anthony spent almost twenty years alone practising his ascetic discipline by, neither going out, nor being often seen by anyone. After a while, many people yearned for his way of life and desired to follow his ascetic practice, and many of his friends came and tore down his door and forced him to come out. When those people saw him they were amazed to see that his body had maintained its natural condition; being neither fat from lack of exercise nor weakened from fasting and fighting with demons. They found him just as they had left him before his withdrawal. The character of his soul was pure, for it had neither been contracted by suffering nor dissipated by pleasure, nor had it been afflicted by laughter or sorrow. Moreover, when Anthony saw the crowd, he was not bothered, nor did he rejoice at so many people greeting him. Instead, like someone guided by reason, he maintained his natural balance.

Through Anthony the Lord healed many who were suffering from bodily illness and purified others of their demons. The Lord gave grace-filled speech to Anthony. He comforted many who mourned and reconciled many. In addition, he preached renunciation of the world in exchange for a life with Christ. He reminded them of the things to come and of God's love for humankind; that God, *"did not spare His Own Son, but delivered Him up for us all"*. Anthony persuaded many to choose the monastic life.

Monastic dwellings came to being in the mountains, and the desert was made a city of monks who left their homes and in turn, registered themselves for citizenship in heaven. He foretold of the greatness of Saint Macarius as well as the persecution the church was to endure in the coming years.

When the day of the departure of Saint Paul drew near, a voice called from heaven to Saint Anthony, telling him that he was not alone in the desert. There was one like him. He was instructed to go and bury his body and his departure was near. Saint Anthony went to Saint Paul and clothed him in a tunic presented to him by Saint Athanasius the Apostolic.

After 105 years of spirituality and purity, the time for Saint Anthony's departure came. He commanded his disciple to hide his body, give his staff to Saint Macarius and give one of his sheepskin cloaks to Saint Athanasius and the other to Anba Serapion. He breathed his last and the angels and saints delivered his spirit into the heavens. His departure is commemorated on 22nd day of the Coptic month of Toba.

SAINT PAUL

Saint Paul was born in Alexandria and had one brother named Peter. When their father departed, they divided the inheritance. Peter took a much larger share of the inheritance and this upset Saint Paul. When he questioned his older brother, he responded saying, "You are a young man, and I am afraid that you might squander it. As for me, I will keep it for you."

They could not reach an agreement that made them both happy so they went to the governor to make a judgement. Along the way, they saw a funeral procession.

Saint Paul asked one of the mourners about the deceased. He found out that he was a noble and rich man but on that day, he was buried with the clothes he was wearing only. All his riches were left behind.

St Paul

Other Names The first hermit

Birth 3rd century AD

Feast February 9/ Amshir 2 (departure)

Saint Paul thought to himself, "What do I have to do then with the money of this temporal world which I shall leave naked?" He turned to his brother and suggested they return home for he no longer even wanted his share of the inheritance. Just as Christ taught us,

"Do not lay up for yourselves treasures on earth, where moth and rust destroy and where thieves break in and steal; 20 but lay up for yourselves treasures in heaven, where neither moth nor rust destroys

and where thieves do not break in and steal. 21 For where your treasure is, there your heart will be also." (Matt **6:19-21**)

On their way back, Saint Paul left his brother and went a different way until he was outside the city. He stayed at a gravesite for three days in prayers and petitions for the Lord's guidance. In the meantime, Saint Paul's brother was searching diligently for him and when he could not find him, he was sorrowful for what he had done.

An angel of the Lord came to Saint Paul and guided him to the eastern inner wilderness where he dwelt for seventy years. During this time, he saw no one. He wore a tunic made of palm tree fiber. A raven would bring him half a loaf of bread each day to sustain him.

When the time of his departure drew near, the Lord wished to reveal the holiness of Saint Paul to Saint Anthony. An angel went to Saint Anthony and told him of Saint Paul. At that time, Saint Anthony thought he was the first to dwell in the desert. The angel said,

"There is a man who lives in the inner wilderness; the world is not worthy of his footsteps. By his prayers, the Lord brings rain and dew to fall on the earth, and bring the flood of the Nile its due season."

When Saint Anthony heard the angel's word, he arose and went into the inner wilderness, a day's walk. He entered Saint Paul's cave and they bowed before each other. On the day that Anthony visited Paul, the raven brought a whole loaf of bread. This signified to Saint Paul that Saint Anthony was truly a man of God as every other day the raven would bring him half a loaf. He instructed him to bring him the tunic of Pope Athanasius that Emperor Constantine had given him.

Saint Anthony went immediately on his way. On his return, he saw the soul of Saint Paul being carried into the heavens. At his arrival, he knew Saint Paul had departed from this world. He kissed him, wept and clothed him in the tunic of Pope Athanasius.

Saint Anthony wanted to bury the body of Saint Paul but he was hindered by two lions who stood by the body of Saint Paul. Anthony knew these were sent from God and so, he knew he should bury the body of the blessed Saint Paul at the place that the lions had marked. He marked the length of the body so that the lions could dig a grave for the precious body of Saint Paul.

Saint Anthony then went to Pope Athanasius and told him what had happened. Saint Athanasius sent for the body of Saint Paul to be brought to him. They could not find the body despite days of searching. Finally Saint Paul appeared to Athanasius in a vision and told him that the Lord would not allow his body to be located. The pope then sent for the return of the men.

The departure of the great Saint Paul is commemorated on the second day of the Coptic month of Amshir.

THE THREE SAINTS ABBA MACARII AND ALL THEIR CHILDREN THE CROSS-BEARERS

Abba Macarius of Egypt

Abba Macarius was born in Lower Egypt around 300AD. He was a monk and hermit and more notably, a father of all monks, earning him the titles of *Macarius the Elder* and the *Lamp of the Desert.* He lived a long life in fear of God and departed to heaven in 391AD.

He was born to God-fearing parents in the Lower Egypt village of Shabsheer, Menuf. His father's name was Abraham and his mother's name was Sarah. They had no sons before Macarius. His father saw in a vision an angel of the Lord proclaiming they would bear a son that would become father to a multitude of spiritual sons.

Surely enough, they had a son and named him Macarius, meaning *blessed.* He was obedient

Abba Macarius of Egypt

Other Names Saint Macarius the Great, Macarius the Elder, The Lamp of the Desert

Birth 300 AD

Feast Baramhat 27/April 5 (departure), Misra 19/August 25 (return of his body to the monastery)

Famous quote "The soul that really loves God and Christ, though it may do ten thousand righteousnesses, esteems itself as having wrought nothing, by reason of its insatiable aspiration after God. Though it should exhaust the body with fastings, with watchings, its attitudes towards the virtues is as if it had not yet even begun to labour for them" to his parents and his God given grace was evident from a young age.

When Macarius grew older, his father forced him to marry. Macarius pretended that he was sick and asked his father if he could go to the wilderness so that he could recover quickly. His father agreed.

While in the wilderness, he prayed to our Lord Christ to direct him according to His divine will. He saw a vision of one of the Cherubim who guided him by the hand to the top of a mountain and showed him the entire desert – from east to west and north to south. The Cherubim told him, "God has given this desert to you and your sons as an inheritance."

Upon his return home, he found that his wife had died. Shortly after, his parents also departed. Macarius blessed the Lord and sold all his goods to the poor. When the people of Shabsheer saw his great charity and compassion for the needy, they requested the Bishop of Ashmoun to ordain him a priest.

Satan saw Macarius growing in virtue and wished to tempt him away from God. A young pregnant girl accused Macarius of defiling her. Macarius accepted the accusation silently. Her family insulted, beat him and inflicted much pain in retaliation. Macarius reproached himself and saw himself as having a wife and child that he now needed to provide for. He worked hard weaving mats and baskets and gave them away to be sold for money for the young girl.

When her delivery drew near, she suffered greatly. For four days, she was in labour. She could not give birth until she confessed Macarius' innocence and named the man that had actually defiled her.

The people who had persecuted Macarius went back to him, begging for his forgiveness. Macarius fled to the Nitran Desert to escape the glory of the world.

He was thirty years old when he entered the desert. He asked an angel to appoint a suitable dwelling place where he could remain. The angel denied his request saying, "Behold all the wilderness is yours, so wheresoever you wish, live there."

St Macarius dwelt in the Inner Desert, in the place of the monastery of St Maximous and Domadious, now known as the monastery of El-Baramous.

He later visited St Anthony the Great who taught him the laws and rules of monasticism. Of St Macarius, St Anthony said that there was no guile in him. St Anthony put the holy eskeem on him that was reserved for anchorites of the desert. St Macarius then returned to his own place in the desert. The number of monks began to increase around him and so he built a church for them.

When word began to spread of the miracles that God performed through him, many kings and emperors sought his help. The daughter of the king of Antioch was brought to him, possessed by an unclean spirit. Macarius quickly healed her. An angel appeared to him and told him to make a place where people who needed healing could come to him. He built a cell and church for himself.

At one point, St Macarius thought there were no righteous people left in the world. A voice from him guided him to a house in Alexandria where two righteous women lived. When he entered, they welcomed him and washed his feet. He found out that these two women had requested from their husbands to become nuns but their husbands refused. They therefore, committed their life to fasting till evening and often with prayers. If either of their sons would cry, they would cater to that son even if he was not their own. They were poor and had only their daily bread for sustenance. The rest they gave to the poor. Having been satisfied that there were still righteous people in the world, Macarius left and returned to the wilderness.

The day of his departure drew near in the year 391AD when he was ninety seven years old. St Anthony and St Bachomious and a company of saints were present at his departure. His departure is commemorated on the 27th of the Coptic Month of Baramhat (April 5).

His disciple, St Babnuda witnessed the great St Macarius' ascension into the heavens. He saw the devils taunting him while he was ascending saying, *"You have conquered us O Macarius."*

St Macarius responded, "I have not conquered you yet."

They continued to taunt him even by to the very gates of heaven. St Macarius would give the same response each time. When he entered the gates of heaven they cried out the same words again but this time he responded, *"Blessed be the Lord Jesus Christ who has delivered me from your hands."*

Before his departure, Saint Macarius commanded his disciples to hide his body. The people of Shabsheer found where his body lay and stole his precious relics and built a church in his honour. His body remained in Shabsheer for 160 years. During the Arab conquest and the rebuilding of his monastery his body was returned.

In honour of Saint Marcarius, Pope Michael V of Alexandria built a large church in the desert of Scetis. He longed to be able to find the body of the great saint so that he could remain forever in their midst.

Elders of the church went to Shabsheer to retrieve his body. They were greeted with swords and sticks to prevent them from taking his body. They left sorrowful. On that night, the governor of the town, saw a vision of St Macarius telling him to allow his children to return his body to its rightful home.

The governor was extremely frightened and requested that the elders return to take his body. They received his body with great joy. The precious body of Saint Macarius was carried on a camel into the desert. The elders refused to rest until the camel stopped at the place where Saint Macarius' body was to be laid. The camel knelt down, licked the body and bowed his head toward the ground. The elders glorified God and buried his body in this place.

Many wonders were performed on that day through the intercessions of St Macarius. We commemorate this on the 19th of the Coptic month of Mesra.

Abba Macarius of Alexandria

Abba Macarius of Alexandria was born in 296AD and lived in the desert from 330AD onwards. He was a disciple of Abba Macarius the Great and was called *Abba Macarius the Junior* for this reason.

Abba Macarius of Alexandria

Other Names Saint Macarius the Junior, Father of the Cells

Birth 296 AD

Feast Bashans 6/May 14 (departure)

He resided in the wilderness near Alexandria and was spiritual guide to many ascetics around him. Many miracles were worked through his hands. He once stayed for five days with his thoughts set on heaven. He thought of early saints, prophets, angels and the Lord Christ. The devils began to fight him after two nights. They would scratch his feet and twist themselves as snakes around his legs. They made his cell appear to be on fire. None of this moved Abba Macarius and they eventually left him. After the fifth day, he had to take care of his needs for life. It is said that this occurred so that he would not be proud of his spiritual achievement.

One day, a hyena pulled him by his garments to lead him to her den. Inside lay three young hyenas that were malformed. The saint was amazed at the intelligence of the hyena. He prayed and lay his hands on them and they were healed. She then brought him a sheep skin that he wore until his departure.

On another occasion, the thought of going to Rome to heal those in need of healing would not leave him. Struggling to remove the thought, he filled a sack of sand and loaded it on himself and walked in the desert until his body was so exhausted that the proud thought left him.

Saint Macarius once received a bunch of fresh grapes. When he wanted to eat them, he saw a monk who was sick and in much greater need so he gave the grapes to him. That monk, wanting to preserve his abstinence, gave the grapes to another monk, who gave them to another. Eventually the grapes returned to St Macarius who praised and gave thanks to God for the abstinence of his disciples.

He went to the monastery of Saint Bakhomious in layman's clothing and remained there for the 40 days of Lent. During this time, he was not seen eating or sitting down. When he made baskets out of palm leaves, he would remain standing. The monks believed him not to be human and asked Saint Bakhomious who Abba Macarius was. The Lord revealed Abba Macarius' identity to Saint Bakhomious who welcomed and received him joyously. Knowing that his identity had been uncovered, Abba Macarius returned to his monastery. There was a period in Alexandria where it did not rain. The Patriarch called Abba Macarius. As soon as Abba Macarius arrived in Alexandria, the rain started and would not stop until he prayed for it to stop.

Emperor Valens exiled Saint Macarius, along with Saint Macarius the Great. While in exile, they guided the people to Christ until they were allowed to return to their monasteries once more.

St Macarius lived a life of miracle performing, healing the sick and casting out devils until the age of 100. In the year 394-395AD, he passed away. His departure is commemorated on the Coptic date of Bashans 6 (May 14).

Abba Macarius, Bishop of Edkow

Little is known about Abba Macarius' early life. He was a very gifted speaker, full of talents and performer of many signs and wonders.

It was said that whenever he preached, the people would weep. His disciples would questions why this was so. He answered saying that when he spoke, he would see the sins of the people and their ungodly works. It is a

Abba Macarius of Edkow

Feast Baba 27/ October 6 (departure)

testament to his great humility and self-denial that the Lord would reveal to him the sins of the people.

On one occasion, he conversed with the Lord at the altar. While the angels were bringing the works of the people, the voice of the Lord came to him saying, *"Why, bishop, are you slack in preaching to your people?"*

Abba Macarius replied, *"My Lord, they do not accept my words."*

"It is meet for the bishop to preach to the people and if they do not accept his words, their blood be upon their own heads."

He was invited to the Council of Chalcedon with Abba Discorus, the 25th Pope of the See of St Mark. He was prevented from entry by the guards because of his modest clothing. When Abba Discorus informed them that he was a bishop, only then did they allow him to enter.

During the Council, Abba Macarius excommunicated the Emperor when he heard the claims made against Christ. He would defend Christ until death.

As a result, he was exiled to the island of Gagra with Abba Discorus. Abba Discorus prophesied that Abba Macarius would become a martyr and sent him back to Alexandria. Upon his arrival, he saw Thomas Lawn, a messenger of King Merkianous preaching the heresy of the two natures of Christ.

The messenger had a decree that stated the two natures of Christ. Abba Macarius refused to sign his name on it. At his refusal, the messenger of the Emperor kicked him and he died instantly because of the frailty of his old age. This fulfilled Abba Discorus' prophesy that he would die a martyr.

It is said that at Abba Macarius' death, the face of the messenger responsible for his death turned to the back and his tongue swelled, choking him and causing his death.

His body was buried at the church of St John the Baptist and Elisha the Prophet. During the burial, a boy that was mute spoke saying that he could see St John the

Baptist and Elisha receiving the saint with great joy. The three bodies were later transferred to the Monastery of St Macari the Great where they can be found today. The church commemorates the departure of St Macarius, bishop of Edco on the 27th of the Coptic month of Babah (Oct. 6).

The bodies of the three saints Macari can be found together at the Monastery of the St Macarius the Great.

Their Children, the Cross-Bearers

The Cross-bearers refers to the monks, hermits and recluses that carry the cross of ascetism. They carry the cross of taking the narrow path to eternal life. They willingly chose to die to the world so that they might feed the soul over the body. They struggled against the desires of the flesh and more so, continual torment from the devils. Some of the confessors and martyrs are also given the title of Cross-bearers.

It is said that the prayers of those in the desert are what keeps the world alive. The Cross bearers escaped the world and all its pleasures for their tremendous love for Christ, our Lord.

In the annual Epsali, a doxology is sung in reverence for the cross-bearers;

"the righteous who perfected their faith, the afflicted and tormented, of whom the world does not deserve. They wander in the wilderness in caves and dens, they are ambassadors for Christ because of their faith and patience. So let us hasten along the path of their struggle towards their perfector Jesus Christ...Intercede on our behalf all the cross-bearers who

perfected their faith in the wilderness, that the Lord may forgive our sins..."

ABBA JOHN THE HEGUMEN

Saint John surnamed Kolobos, that is "little" or "dwarf," was among the most eminent saints that inhabited the desert of Scetes. He was born in the Upper Egypt town of Tebsa about the year 339 AD to a poor but holy family. Sine his early years, his desire for monastic life led him to remote places where he trained himself for this ascetic lifestyle. It was not long before he was led by Divine inspiration to leave his town. At the age of 18, he retired into the wilderness of Scetes and set himself with his whole heart to put on the spirit of Christ.

In the wilderness of Scetis, Abba John yearned for the holy, angelic garments of monasticism and thus sought out an experienced elder, Abba Pemouah. Abba John offered Abba Pemouah a metania and asked him to live with him in the wilderness. Abba Pemouah wished to

Abba John the Hegumen

Other Names Abba John the dwarf, Abba John the short

Birth 339 AD

Feast October 30/Baba 20 (departure).

Famous Quote "Even if we are entirely despised in the eyes of men, let us rejoice that we are honoured in the sight of God."

Abba John said, "Who sold Joseph?"

A brother replied saying, 'It was his brethren.' The old man said to him, 'No, it was his humility which sold him, because he could have said, "I am their brother" and have objected, but, because he kept silence, he sold himself by his humility. It is also his humility which set him up as chief in Egypt.'"

test Abba John and said to him; *"My son, it is not right for you to dwell here, for this is a toilsome desert where the inhabitants work with their hands and sleep on the ground. They have many fasts and prayers and great tribulations. Why don't you return to the world and live well?"*

To this Abba John replied; *"If God wills, my father, do not turn me away, for I came to live in obedience to you and under the shadow of your prayers. If you don't accept me now, I hope that the Lord will incline your heart towards me."*

Abba Pemouah, who never made a hasty decision, took time to ask the Lord Christ to clarify the matter of John to him. Thus an angel of the Lord appeared to him saying, *"The Lord says unto you, 'Accept this brother for he will be chosen unto us.'"* With this answer, Abba Pemouah went to John and shaved his head, he took the monastic garments and prayed over them for three days and three nights. After this, the angel of the Lord appeared again and sealed the garments for Abba John's use. Abba John began a life of great asceticism and holy works.

One day, Abba Pemouah decided to give Abba John another test, so he kicked out Abba John saying, *"I cannot live with you."* Abba John stayed seven days in front of the door, showing his loyalty without anger or violent reaction. Each day, Abba Pemouah would go out and hit John with a reed and Abba John would offer Pemouah a metania. On the seventh day of this trial period, Abba Pemouah, while in church, saw a vision of seven angels holding seven crowns destined for the head of Abba John. With this sign, Abba Pemouah took

Abba John back to live with him in mutual honour and reverence.

After some time, Abba Pemouah found a dry branch and gave it to Abba John, saying, *"Take this and water it."* Abba John obeyed by watering the branch every day, which entailed a 20km journey to the water and 20km again back home. After three years of persistent watering, the branch grew and became a fruitful tree. Abba Pemouah picked some of the fruit and took it to other elders, saying, *"Take, eat from the fruit of obedience."*

Later, Abba Pemouah was sick for 12 years and Abba John served him in submission, without grumbling or complaining. On his death bed, Abba Pemouah gathered the elders and took John's hand, prayed and said, *"Take care of this person, for he is an angel and not human."* He commanded Abba John to live by the tree of obedience and then passed away.

After his years of obedience to Abba Pemouah, Abba John was blessed with the discipleship of his own elder brother, who had become a monk, and was appointed a hegumen over the church. While the patriarch was laying his hands upon John's head during his ordination, a voice from heaven was heard by all, saying, *"Worthy, worthy, worthy."* At every liturgy, Abba John could perceive who was worthy of receiving communion and who was not.

Later in his life, while Abba John was resting in his cell, a brother entered and saw angels hovering over him in his sleep, each saying, *"Let me place my wings over him."*

After some time, the Barbarians invaded the wilderness of Scetes. Abba John left for the mountain of St. Anthony -not out of fear but, as he said, *"Lest a Barbarian comes to kill me and goes to hell on my account; I do not want to be at peace and another in torture on my account. Even if he is not like me at worship, he is my brother in the human image."*

After leaving the desert, Abba John lived alone as a faithful and God fearing servant on the suburbs of a town. When the end of his life neared, God sent the pure saints Abba Macarius the Great and Abba Anthony to comfort Saint John and inform him of his coming departure. When he drew near his end, his disciples entreated him to leave them some final lesson of Christian perfection. He sighed, and that he might shun the air of a teacher alleging his own doctrine and practice he said, ``*I never followed my own will; nor did I ever teach another what I had not first practised myself."*

Abba John then fell ill and sent his servant to complete a duty in town. Then angels and saints gathered to receive the soul of the blessed Abba John, ascending with him into the Heavens. When the servant returned, he saw the soul of the saint surrounded by the congregation of saints and angels, singing in front of Abba John; and before them all was one like the sun, praising God. The servant was astonished, so an angel came to him and told him the name of each saint, pointing at each with his finger. The servant said to the angel, *"Who is that one in front who shines like the sun?"*

The angel replied, *"That is Saint Anthony, father of all monks."* When the servant arrived at the cell, he found Abba John kneeling; the great saint had given over his soul while kneeling. The servant mourned greatly and hurried into the city to tell the townspeople, who came and carried Abba John with great honour, witnessing many miracles by the power of his body. The monks buried Abba John the Short, leaving his soul free to receive all who seek his aid. He departed on the 20th day of the Coptic month of Baba in the year 405 AD.

Saint Anba Bishoy

Saint Bishoy was born in the town of Shansa, Egypt, in 320 AD. He lived a life of servitude to the Lord. Most notably, he is attributed for carrying Christ and washing the feet of Christ. He lived his final days on Mount Ansana. He is venerated in both the Oriental and Eastern Orthodox churches.

Anba Bishoy was the youngest of six brothers. His mother had a vision of an angel who told her, "*The Lord says to you, 'give Me one of your children to serve Me.'*"

She answered, "*Lord take whoever you want.*"

The angel chose the thin and frail Bishoy to which his mum responded, "*My Lord, take one who is strong to serve the Lord.*"

The angel responded, "*This is the one whom the Lord has chosen.*"

Abba Bishoy

Other Names the righteous, perfect man, the beloved of our Saviour, the star of the desert.

Birth 320 AD

Feast July 15/Abib 8 (departure)

Famous quote "I have a Trinity, and everything I do is like the Trinity"

At the age of 20, Saint Bishoy entered the wilderness of Scetes and was ordained a monk by Saint Bemwah, who was also a spiritual father of Saint John the Dwarf.

After the departure of Saint Bemwah, Saint Bishoy resided in the present site of the monastery of Saint Bishoy as a hermit. Saint Bishoy struggled much in asceticism and many worships. Many monks would gather around him, compelled by his love, wisdom, simplicity and kindness.

Saint Bishoy's asceticism was extreme; he would tie his hands and hair with a rope attached to the ceiling so that he would not sleep during his nights of prayer.

There was an ascetic old man that lived on the mountain of Ansena that would guide many younger monks. He made a claim that the Holy Spirit was not God and deceived many by his words. When Anba Bishoy heard his, he weaved a basket of three ears and visited the old man. The old man and his followers asked him why he had weaved three ears on to the basket. He responded, "I have a Trinity, and everything I do is like the Trinity."

From there, he was able to explain the theology of the Holy Spirit and the Trinity. They were convinced and returned to the true faith. Anba Bishoy returned to his monastery in Scetes.

Saint Bishoy saw our Lord and Saviour on numerous occasions. When his fellow monks asked him to plead to our Lord to appear to them as well, he told them that Jesus would meet them at the top of a mountain. On their way up the mountain, they all out-ran Anba Bishoy, passed an Older Monk who was struggling to climb. Anba Bishoy saw the Old Man and carried Him on his shoulders. Gradually, he felt the weight of the monk decrease as he climbed. When he realised that the older monk was in fact Jesus Christ, he said, "My Lord, heaven is too small for You and the earth trembles at Your glory. How can a sinner like me carry You?" Because of his great love, he was promised that his body would never see corruption. When Anba Bishoy reached the other monks, he told them that Christ had already appeared but they failed to recognise him.

Another time, he was visited by Christ in his cell. He saw a stranger that appeared weary from walking. He invited the stranger into his cell and washed his feet. While he was washing his feet, the stranger said, "*My chosen Bishoy! You are an honourable man.*" Realising that it was the Lord's feet that he was washing, he knelt down and worshipped Him.

When the Barbarians invaded the wilderness of Scetes, he left and resided on Mount Ansena until his departure. His departure is commemorated on the 8th day of the Coptic month of Abib.

In 842 AD, after the time of persecution had ended, his body was relocated to his monastery in the wilderness of Scetes.

SAINT PAUL OF TAMOUH AND EZEKIEL HIS
DISCIPLE

Saint Paul of Tamouh was a contemporary of Saint Bishoy, the Beloved of our Gracious Saviour and wished to imitate his love for Christ. From an early age, he lived the words of King Solomon when he said, *"Remember your Creator in the days of your youth, before the difficult days come and the years arrive when you say, 'I have no will to face them'"* (Ecclesiastes 12:1). As a youth the saint desired to live a solitary life, and went to mount Ansena to pursue this desire of his heart which was to live completely for Christ. There he was accompanied by his disciple Ezekiel, who witnessed Abba Paula's great love for the Lord and many virtues.

Saint Paul was also extremely devout in his asceticism. It was well known that he pushed his body beyond what many of us would consider normal; always striving in prayer and fasting even when he was exhausted, all out of his great love for our Lord Jesus Christ. He constantly forsook the needs and desires of the flesh for the sake of spiritual nourishment and growth. HH Pope Shenouda III commented on this saying, *"St. Paul of Tamouh tired himself*

St Paul of Tamouh

Feast Baba 7/ October 17 (departure)

Famous Quote "What is my labour compared to all your labours, O Lord, for our salvation? It is better for us to weary ourselves here on earth and attain crowns of struggle than to have rest here and be tired in eternity" *in asceticism till our Lord Jesus Christ appeared to him saying, "Leave off labour, my beloved Paul." But the saint replied, "What is my labour compared to all your labours, O Lord, for our salvation!" It is better for us to weary ourselves here on earth and attain crowns of struggle than to have rest here and be tired in eternity"*

Abba Paul possessed virtues of patience and longsuffering, striving to work hard here on earth for the sake of the heavenly glories that would await him at his departure. As he grew older, he eventually was led by the Lord to meet the beloved Saint Bishoy who was living on Mount Ansena after fleeing the Barbarians that had taken hold of the wilderness of Scetes. Our Lord Jesus Christ spoke to Abba Paul, telling him: *"Your body will be buried with that of My chosen Bishoy."*

Saint Paul of Tamouh departed in peace in the year 415 AD. His departure is commemorated on the 7th day of the Coptic month of Baba. Little is recorded about his disciple Ezekiel but he is also remembered through the life of Saint Paul of Tamouh.

Approximately 400 years after their departure, on the 13th of December 841 AD, Pope Joseph the 1st wanted to fulfil one of Saint Bishoy's wishes which was to move his blessed body along with Abba Paul to Saint Bishoy's Monastery in the wilderness of Scetes.

When they first tried moving the saints' bodies, they attempted to carry Saint Bishoy's body alone on a boat across the Nile. The boat remained absolutely still beyond their control until they brought Saint Paul of Tamouh's body along as well, thus the Lord's promise that they would rest together was fulfilled. Today their bodies lie in the main Church of the Monastery of St Bishoy in the Wadi El Natrun desert.

Saints Maximous and Domadious

Saints Maximous and Domadious were sons of the Roman Emperor, Walendianous. Walendianous loved our Lord Jesus Christ and brought up his sons steadfast in the faith. From a young age, Maximos and Domadious displayed great zeal for Christ and were holy and Christian in manner.

When they realised that this world and all it has to offer is only temporal, they wanted to pursue monastic living. They asked their father if they could travel to the city of Nicea where the first Eucenenical council was held in 325AD. Upon arrival, they sent messengers back to their parents to let them know that they had decided to stay there.

Sts Maximous and Domadious

Feast Toba 14/January 22 (departure of Saint Maximous)

Toba 17/ January 25 (departure of Saint Domadious)

They made their desire to become monks known to a monk in Nicea but he feared their father and so, sent them to Saint Agabius in Syria. They stayed with Saint Agaibus for six years learning the monastic way until his departure. Saint Agaibus commanded them to go to Saint Macarius whom he had only seen in the spirit and not in the flesh and he would guide them.

Saint Maximous and Domatious grew in virtue and humility and were granted the gift of healing. News quickly spread to the surrounding counties, especially among sea merchants. One of their father's stewards saw a sail boat with, "Maximous and Domatious" written on its sail. Their mother and sister quickly travelled to meet them. Upon their arrival, Maximous and Domatious recognised them immediately and wept. They conforted them despite being unwilling to return home.

When the Patriarch of Rome departed, the people wished to ordain Saint Maximos in his place. This came as a great joy to their family but Maximos remembered the command of Saint Agaibus and both disguised themselves and fled along the Mediterranean river toward Scetes. When they were thirsty, God transformed the salty water to fresh water.

They finally reached the wilderness of Scetes and asked Saint Macarius if they could be his disciples. Saint Macarius was hesitant because he knew they were rich and though they would struggle in the desert. They told him to test them and if they failed, they would leave. Saint Macarius gave them a shovel and told them to dig a cave for themselves in a solid rock. He thought this would tire them and they would leave. Seeing that they completed this task, he taught them how to plait leaves and someone who they could sell their produce to, and then left them.

Three years passed and Saint Maximous and Domatious continued to live in the wilderness of Scetes, not meeting anyone and only going to church on Sunday to partake of Holy Communion. Saint Macarius marvelled that they did not seek his advice at that time. He spent a week in prayer, wanting to know the secret behind the asceticism of these two great saints. He then went to visit them in their cell and spent the night with them.

That night, Saint Macarius awoke at midnight to complete his prayers and found that Saint Maximous and Domatious were already awake and praying. He saw a ray of light like fire coming from their mouths toward heaven. He saw devils swarming around them like flies but the angel of the Lord was standing with a sword for their defence. At dawn, they pretended to be asleep and awoke the same time as Saint Macarius. Saint Macarius asked them to pray for him, so they bowed down before him while remaining silent.

It pleased the Lord to take them away from this world and shortly Saint Maximous became ill. They sent to Saint Macarius to come to visit him. Saint Macarius arrived and found him still sick. He saw legions of prophets and saints, among them Saint John the Baptist, all surrounding the bed where Saint Maximous lay. Saint Maximous gave up his spirit shortly and was received by the heavenly hosts. Saint Maximous departed on the 14th day of the Coptic month of Tobah.

Saint Domatious wept bitterly at the departure of his beloved brother and begged Saint Macarius to pray that he could with his brother in heaven. Three days later, Saint Domatious suffered the same fever and Saint Macarius returned to him. On his way, he saw a crowd of saints outside the cave. By this, he knew that Saint Domatious had departed. His departure is commemorated on the 17th day of the month of Tobah. Saints Maximous and Domatious became the first monks to depart from the wilderness of Scetes. Saint

Macarius built a church where the Saints resided. Today,
it is known as the monastery, "El Baramous."

THE 49 MARTYRS

The wilderness of Scetes was home to many monks that fled the world to be united with Christ. From the earliest times of Saint Anthony and Saint Paul to Saint Macarius, Saint Maximous and Domatius, Abba Isidore the Priest, Saint Moses the Strong and the Cross-bearers that fought the good fight of faith, the wilderness of Sheheet was a blessed place. Over the centuries, the wilderness of Sheheet and its blessed inhabitants underwent various attacks from Berbers that sought to kill and destroy them.

During the fifth century AD, Emperor Theodosius the Less reigned. He was a Christian emperor that showed compassion for the Christian people of Egypt. He was without a son and this upset him greatly. He wrote to the elders of Sheheet to pray that God grants him a son. Saint Isidore replied to him saying, "God will not allow for you to have a son that will participate in the heretics after him."

The Emperor read the message and gave thanks to God. The people began to advise him to marry another wife so that through her, he may gain offspring to carry on the empire after him. The Emperor liked this idea

The 49 Martyrs

Other Names The Elders of Sheheet

Feast Tobah 26/Feb 3 (departure), Amishir 5/Feb 12

Famous Quote "I see spiritual beings putting crowns on the heads of the elders. I shall go and receive a crown like them" – Zius, son of Martinos.

but did not want to do anything without the approval of the elders.

In 444 AD, he sent Martinos to speak with the elders of Sheheet. Martinos went to Sheheet and also took his son, Zius, so that he may receive their blessings. When they arrived at Scetes, Abba Isidore had passed away so the elders took Martinos and Zius to his body. They called to Abba Isidore saying, "Our father, we have received a letter from the Emperor. What shall we say to him?"

A voice came from the body saying, "What I had said before, I also say now, the Lord will never give him a son to participate with the heretics, even if he marries ten women."

Upon hearing the word, Martinos and his son wished to return. As they were leaving, pagan Berbers attacked the monastery. Anba Yuannis called upon the brethren saying, "The Berbers have come to kill. Whoever among you would like to become martyr, let him stand, whoever is afraid, let him hide in the palace."

Some of the brethren hid but 49 remained and were killed by the berbers. Martinos and his son hid and watched while the 49 were martyred. Zius looked up and saw angels placing crowns of glory on the elders. He told his father that he wanted to go so that he may receive a crown of glory with them. Martinos also wished to go with him. They came out of hiding and revealed themselves to the berbers. They were killed and also received crowns of martyrdom.

When the Berbers left, the monks that were hiding in the palace returned and took the bodies and placed them in a cave. The body of Zius was later stolen by the people of El-Fayoum. When they arrived at El-Fatyoum, an angel of the Lord appeared to them and returned the body of Zius to his father. There were several attempts to separate the bodies of Zius and Martinos but to no avail. In a vision one night, one of the fathers heard a voice saying, *"Praise God, we were not separated in the flesh, nor are we separated when we are with Christ. Why do you want to separate our bodies?"*

The attacks on the monastery continued through the years and the bodies of the elders of Sheheet were re-located to a cave beside the church of Saint Macarius the Great in 538 AD. Pope Theodosius, 33rd Patriarch of the See of Saint Mark built a church for them.

Later, in the 18th century, Ibrahim El-Gohary built a church in their honour that exists till this day in the monastery of Saint Macarius. "The cell of the 49" still holds their precious bodies also. The 49 elders of Sheheet are commemorated on the 26th day of the Coptic month of Tobah.

Anba Benjamin, the 38th Patriarch of the See of Saint Mark established the 5th day of the Coptic month of Amshir to commemorate the relocation of the bodies to their current home in the cave at the monastery of Saint Macarius.

SAINT ABBA MOSES

Saint Moses was born in 330 AD Ethiopia. Little is known of Saint Moses' early life. He lived a life as a slave to the people, worshipping the sun. He was a strong and mighty man who would eat and drink in excess. He committed all kinds of crimes including murder and robbery. He was undefeatable and feared by many.

He would lift his eyes to the sun on many occasions and demand the sun to prove that it was god to no avail. When he realised that the sun was not god, he prayed to God to reveal Himself to him.

Abba Moses

Other Names Saint Moses the Strong

Birth 330 AD

Feast Paona 24/ July 1 (martyrdom)

Famous quote "It is better for a man to put himself to death rather than his neighbour, and he should not condemn him in anything"

One day, he was told that the monks of Wadi E-Natroun knew the true God. He instantly arose, girded his sword and went to the wilderness of Scetes.

He met Saint Isidore the priest who was afraid when he first saw this large and mighty man. Saint Moses comforted him and told him that he just wanted to know more about God. Saint Isidore guided him to Saint Macarius the Great who preached to him, taught him the faith and baptised him at the monastery of Saint Bishoy.

Saint Moses fought relentlessly against the devil and his former ways. He was initially guided by immense zeal for monastic life but quickly became discouraged as he believed he would never attain spiritual perfection. Early in the morning, Abba Isidore the priest took him to a high mountain to watch the sunrise and said, *"Only slowly do the rays of the sun drive away the night and usher in a new day, and thus, only slowly does one become a perfect contemplative."*

It was said of Anba Moses that while the other monks slept, he would take their water pots and fill them with water from a well that was located a long way away from the monastery.

His wisdom and humility became widespread. It was once said that the monks had come together to condemn a brother for his sin. Saint Moses was asked to join the council to convict this monk. He went to the council carrying a bag of sand that was open on one end. The monks were perplexed and asked him why. He responded, *"this sand is my sins which are trailing out behind me, while I go to judge the sins of another."*

After many years of failed attempts, the devil harmed Anba Moses by causing a sore on his foot that made him bed-ridden. When Anba Moses realised this was from the devil, he persisted even more in his spiritual struggles, increasing in ascetism and worship until his skin became like burnt wood. God looked upon Anba with compassion and removed from him all illness and pain.

As he grew in virtue and asceticism, many monks would be drawn to him until he became a spiritual guide of 500 brothers. The brothers elected and ordained him a priest.

When the day of his ordination came, the Patriarch, wishing to test him, said, *"Who brought this black man here? Cast him out."*

Anba Moses left in obedience and thought it was a punishment for his former life and misconduct. The patriarch was quick to call him back and ordained him a priest and said to him, *"Moses, all of you have become altogether white."*

In 405 AD, he went with some elders to Saint Macarius the Great who prophesied that one of them would die by martyrdom. Saint Moses thought it would be him as it says, "For all who take the sword will perish by the sword" (Matt 25:52). Upon their return to the monastery, the Barbarians entered and took hold of the monastery. He told his brethren to escape but he would remain, for his time had come. The Barbarians killed him with seven other brothers. One of the brothers that was in hiding saw the angel of the Lord with a crown in his hand, waiting for the beloved Anba Moses. He went out from his hiding place and received the crown of martyrdom.

Saint Moses is venerated in the Coptic Orthodox church, along with the Oriental and Eastern Orthodox and Catholic churches because of the transforming power of repentance. His body was laid next to the body of Saint Isidore the priest and it continues to provide blessing in the Monastery of El-Baramous. His martyrdom is

remembered on the 24th day of the Coptic month of
Paona.

SAINT JOHN KAME

Saint John Kame was a pious monk, desert dweller, priest and father of the community. He was born in Sais, Egypt in the 4th century AD. He was very renown for establishing key holy communities and monasteries in various locations. He chose the path of celibacy despite being married to his wife on the conditions of his parents. He was pure in both single life devotion and married life devotion. He crucified his flesh, in mind and in deed, and taught others to do the same and was teacher and encourager for the salvation of souls.

St John Kame

Other Names John Kame the priest

Birth 4th century AD

Feast Kiahk 25/ January 3 (departure)

Famous Quote "Do not hold disputations regarding heresies, neither go into a house with women, nor put your trust in rulers, nor get for yourselves substance, but let your handiwork suffice you."

Saint John Kame excelled in every virtue and performed good deeds in secrets He was zealous in virtue, sober in his judgement, sanctified in his soul, good toward all men, a lover of charity and strangers and devout in faith. He was diligent in going early to Church, fasting at all times, praying and meditating fervently day and night, keeping his body in subjection and withdrawing himself from all worldly cares

His parents arranged for a young virgin to be betrothed to him, and finally the wedding was accomplished that he should take her as wife. After the marriage ceremony, while St John was in the chamber with his wife, the righteous man spread out his hands praying,

"Grant me my Lord that I may be in the purity of virginity unto the end and grant thy servant also [his wife] that she may be granted the lot of the five wise virgins. Instead of the bride chamber of this world, we should be made worthy of the bride chamber that is in heaven; in exchange for the children that we should beget in flesh, we shall become the children of God and the companions of his angels."

After these things happened, a marvel occurred where God commanded a vine to spring up in the bride chamber which bore much fruit spreading in the whole house (as a symbol of their purity). When his wife saw this, she marvelled and blessed him. She herself went into a convent to become a nun, while he went to a monastery seeking to be a monk.

As his piety increased, Saint John was no stranger to angels' appearances, in which a man of light appeared to him instructing him to visit the monastery of Scetes (where Abba Macarius resided) to become a monk. After some time in the monastery, another angel appeared to confirm his inheritance amongst the desert fathers, a ministry of work, and leadership over souls.

Saint John then moved to reside in a cave. He was very strict in his piety and desert life. His eating regimen was minimal, often only eating between Sabbath to Sabbath, and at times not eating for forty days straight.

He would only go to sleep briefly, resting his head against a wall.

This diligence was rewarded by an honourable visit from the Virgin Saint Mary who promised him that the land he was currently living on would become a holy community and the protection of the Lord will be upon it.

"I will establish my covenant with thee and I will preserve my mercy for thee; for I will abide in this place with thee, because I love it; and it shall become for thee a holy community, and there shall be unto thee multitudes of children and they shall call it by my name; and the blessing of my Son and His peace and His protection shall abide in thy community. The angels shall visit the monastery and shall watch over the children that no traitor shall break through the walls of thy dwelling place forever."

She gave him three gold artefacts to be used as a blessing for the community. A monastery was built in his honour which attracted many monks and many children of God. St Athanasius also appeared to him and praised him for his *"sweet smelling prayers which have reached the presence of God as a remembrance for thee for ever and thy name shall endure to all generations"*, and promised him blessings, protection and success with his community.

Saint John was eventually consecrated against his will as a priest and was instructed by an angel to then relocate to South Egypt to minister there. During this time, his piety attracted much attention and many people became a community in his name. St John, while standing before the sanctuary, would see the glory of God came upon the altar as if it were fire.

In his final days, it pleased the Lord to grant him rest from all his burdens and was visited by a fever. Saint John gave his monastic community members last words of exhortation on how to manage effectively, *"Do not hold disputations regarding heresies, neither go into a house with women, nor put your trust in rulers, nor get for yourselves substance, but let your handiwork suffice you"* and when he looked up, he saw a glorious entourage of angels and saints (as well as other desert dwellers in the past), and his soul was transferred to heaven. He received the prizes and high rewards of the saints and an inheritance in the Heavenly Jerusalem. His body was enshrouded with great honour and dispersed sweet odours like spices. A notable monument was built over his tomb where he rests till this day. His departure is commemorated on the 25th day of the Coptic month of Kiahk.

ABBA DANIEL THE HEGUMEN

Abba Daniel was an Archpriest of the wilderness of Scetes. He was closely associated with Saint Anastasia, who disguised herself as a monk till her departure. He was known as the perfect and pure father and guided many monks through the path of righteousness.

Abba Daniel the Hegumen

Other Names the Hegomen, the Archpriest, Abba Daniel of Sheheet

Birth 6th century AD

Feast Bashons 8/May 16 (departure)

Famous Quote "The body prospers in the measure in which the soul is weakened, and the soul prospers in the measure in which the body is weakened."

While little is known of Abba Daniel's early life, he had a large impact while in the wilderness of Scetes. His prayers were continually heard and answered by our Lord and many flocked to Abba Daniel to imitate our Saviour through him.

One day he saw a person by the name of Olagi who was by trade, a stone cutter for gold. Olagi would take a very small portion of gold and would live by this alone and the rest of his wealth he would distribute to the poor. Abba Daniel prayed that Olagi would receive greater wealth so that his deeds of mercy would increase. God answered Abba Daniel's prayers and with Olagi's new found profit, he travelled to Constantinople and became a minister of the Emperor. He quickly forsook his deeds of mercy.

Abba Daniel heard this and was deeply saddened. He travelled to Constantinople to return the lost soul of Olagi. While in Constantinople, he saw our Lord Christ in a vision. Abba Daniel was being commanded to crucifixion by the people. Jesus demanded the lost soul of Olagi. When Abba Daniel woke up, he entreated our Lord to bring back Olagi to his former state. Soon after, the Emperor passed away and was succeeded by a new Emperor who sent Olagi away and took all his wealth. Olagi escaped the wrath of the new Emperor and returned to his former life, cutting stone. Abba Daniel met with him and told him what had happened.

Saint Anastasia, or *Anastasius*, as she was known by the other monks, resided in a cell near Abba Daniel for twenty eight years. Only Abba Daniel knew that she was a female and the daughter of a highly-regarded Emperor. When the time of her departure drew near, she wrote on a piece of pottery, that was to be received by Abba Daniel that she wanted him to bury her body. Her final request was that she be buried with her clothes on so that the other monks would not recognise her as a female. They prayed and and buried her. The monk that carried her body recognised that she could not be a male. He marvelled in silence and later asked Abba Daniel to reveal her story to him.

When the time of Abba Daniel's departure drew near, he gathered the monks around him. He comforted them, strengthened their faith and departed in peace. His departure is commemorated on the 8th day of the Coptic month of Basons.

SAINT ABBA ISIDORE

Little is known of our father, Abba Isidore the Priest. Abba Isidore is most prominently known as a companion of Saint Macarius the Great and the spiritual guide of Saint Moses the Strong.

Abba Isidore fled from the world and resided in the wilderness of Scetes. It is believed that he was head of one of the four main communities. Abba Isidore is well known for his gift of healing. Many with various diseases and illness were brought to him and he cured them through the grace of God.

While in the wilderness of Scetes, Abba Isidore attracted many great monks, including Saint Moses the Strong. At their first meeting, Abba Isidore was afraid of the large and mighty stature of Anba Moses but when Anba Moses explained his situation, he grew close to him and guided him to the

Abba Isidore

Other Names Abba Isidore the priest

Birth 2nd-3rd century AD

Feast Paone 24 / July 1 (departure)

Famous Quote "Of all evil suggestions, the most terrible is that of following one's own heart, that is to say, one's own thought, and not the law of God. A man who does this will be afflicted later on, because he has not recognized the mystery, and he has not found the way of the saints in order to work in it. For now is the time to labour for the Lord, for salvation is found in the day of affliction: for it is written: 'By your endurance you will gain your lives" means of repentance. He introduced Anba Moses to Saint Macarius the Great.

When Anba Moses was struggling against a particular sin, he confided in Abba Isidore who said, *"Look towards the West.' So he looked carefully in that direction and saw a host of demons provoking confusion and causing disturbance with their warmongering. Then Abba Isidore said again: 'Now look towards the East.' When he turned to the East, Abba Moses saw countless hosts of Holy Angels surrounded in glory. The Elder then said to Moses: 'There! These that you see are the ones the Lord sends to help the Saints who struggle; but the ones that you saw previously in the West are those who make war on them. Our allies, therefore, are greater in number. This is why you should have courage and not be afraid.' After this, Abba Moses gave thanks to God, took courage, and returned to his cell."*

When this great saint was growing older, Abba Poeman told him to rest but Abba Isidore responded saying, *"Even if Isidore were burned, and his ashes thrown to the winds, I would not allow myself any relaxation because the Son of God came here for our sake."*

Abba Isidore would flee from all temptation, to the extent that even the demons were frightened of him and dared not approach his peaceful presence where anger could never find its place. He once journeyed to Alexandria to meet with the archbishop and upon his return, the brethren asked him what was happening in the city. He responded saying that the only face he saw was the face of the archbishop whom he had gone to meet. This disturbed the brethren but Abba Isidore later clarified saying, "the thought of looking at anyone did not get the better of me." This displayed his immense strength and guard against all sins that may befall his eyes.

Abba Isidore would greet his brethren saying, "Forgive your brother, so that you also may be forgiven." He was determined to have his will aligned with the will of our Almighty God and would say, "It is the wisdom of the saints to recognize the will of God. Indeed, in obeying the truth, man surpasses everything else, for he is the image and likeness of God."

Abba Isidore departed in peace around 391 AD. He remains a beacon of hope, light and asceticism to the nations till this day.

ABBA PACHOM AND TADROS HIS DISCIPLE

Abba Pachom (Bakhomious) was known as the, "father of community." He earned this title from his establishment of communal monastic life. In modern times, this is known as coenobitic life.

Abba Pachom was born in the year 292 AD to pagan parents who forced him to worship idols. He rejected their orders and mocked idolatry. In 310 AD he was recruited by the Roman army. With many other recruits, Bakhomious was taken by boat along the River Nile to Thebes – a place where many Christians dwelt. Upon arriving into the city they were placed into its prisons for the night. The Christians of Thebes were moved with compassion towards the ill-treated soldiers so they brought them food, water and showed them great love. This was the first contact of St. Pachomious with Christianity. Such uncommon, selfless love left such a great impression that he was compelled to learn and follow Jesus Christ.

Abba Pachom

Other Names Father of community

Birth 292 AD

Feast Bashons 14/ May 22 (departure)

Famous Quote "Though abstinence and prayer be of great merit, yet sickness suffered with patience is of much greater."

Some time later, the Emperor was overthrown and the army was dismantled. Bakhomious retreated to a small village, Seneset, with a known Christian church, called Chenoboscium, where he entered and participated with the catechumens (those preparing for baptism). He settled in a place outside the village, and grew vegetables to feed himself and any strangers who should happen to pass by. He learnt the doctrine and was baptised in this church. Bakhomious commonly prayed, *"O God, Creator of heaven and earth, cast on me an eye of pity, deliver me from my miseries. Teach me the true way of pleasing you, and it shall be the whole employment, and most earnest study of my life to serve you, and to do your will."*

After Bakhomious was baptised a serious epidemic struck the village. He found this as an opportunity to serve the sick, pray and thought about how he would most faithfully follow Christ and attain the great end. The charity and charm of Bakhomious attracted many people who made their dwelling near him. However, he longed for solitude and thought of becoming a hermit. After spending 3 years in the desert he found an elderly man named, Balamon, who served God in the desert with perfection. Bakhomious begged that Balamon would accept him under his guidance however, Balamon advised Bakhomious to try living in a monastery to understand the difficulties in the life he was seeking. He explained, *"Consider my son, that my diet is only bread and salt. I drink no wine, use no oil, watch one half of the night, spending that time in singing psalms, or in meditating on the Holy Scripture, and sometimes pass the whole night without sleeping."*

Bakhomious was amazed at this account, but not discouraged, and Balamon agreed to teach him. Balamon and Bakhomious prayed the psalms together. They exercised in manual labour, whilst praying internally so that they may occupy their hands and assist the needy. Above all things, Bakhomious prayed for perfect purity of heart, that being disengaged from all secret attachments to the world, he might love God with all his affections. He often prayed with arms outstretched, in the form of the cross, which was a posture much used by the church at that time.

Initially he would be tired at night, in the times of prayer, but Balamon would urge him saying, *"Labour and watch my dear Pachomious, lest the enemy overthrow you and ruin all your endeavours."* Just as our Lord Jesus told his disciples, *"watch and pray, lest you enter into temptation."* To overcome this, Bakhomious would occasionally carry bags of sand from one place to another to quench his tiredness.

The young Bakhomious had the custom of meditating while he was walking across the neighbouring uninhabited desert. One day, led by the Holy Spirit, he walked along the Nile River till he reached the village of Tabenna. There he heard a voice: *"Bakhomious, struggle, dwell in this place and build a monastery, for many will come to you to become monks."*

He was then given the instructions for the communal monastic life. St. Bakhomious built a monastery there around the year 325 AD; roughly 20 year after Saint Anthony established his first monastery, also at the time of Saint Athanasius and the council of Nicea. The monastery quickly grew, reaching over 100 monks. It was this way that the cenobotic- communal monasticism was born.

Saint Bakhomious was strict with the community of monks that began to grow around him. They practised silence, so that among a great multitude, a person seemed to be in solitude. Novices were tried severely before being accepted into the monastery. The monks were kept occupied in various manual labours, not allowing a moment for idleness. In travelling from one place to another, the monks were encouraged to meditate on a passage from the Holy Scripture and to sing psalms

The Holy Spirit was manifested in Saint Bakhomious through various gifts, including the gifts of faith, healing, working of miracles, and his wisdom and knowledge in teaching. He would tell those who approached him in illness that it was a result of divine goodness and he would pray for their comfort.

Saint Bakhomious was ill for a while, however, he never complained or tried to inform anyone of his illness. When his disciple would ask Bakhomious to pray for his health, he would respond, "*Though abstinence and prayer be of great merit, yet sickness suffered with patience is of much greater merit.*" He suffered from a common disease that had become endemic in Upper Egypt. During this time, it killed over one hundred monks. He endured this difficult time with great patience and cheerfulness; he peacefully died around the year 348AD and departed into the heavens. His departure is commemorated on 14th day of the Coptic month of Bashons.

Tadros his disciple

Saint Theodore (Tadros) was the disciple of Saint Bakhomious. While still young, Saint Theodore became a monk. Anba Bakhomious taught him the coenobitic lifestyle. He displayed extraordinary obedience and became a guide to the younger monks. When Saint Bakhomious departed, he delegated Saint Theodore to replace him. Saint Theodore followed closely in the footsteps of Saint Bakhomious, ensuring that communal monasticism remained steadfast till this very day.

Saint Theodore lived a long life in devotion to our Lord and Saviour Jesus Christ. He departed in peace surrounded by the monks that looked up to him. His departure is commemorated on the second day of the Coptic month of Bashons.

Saint Abba Shenoute the Archimandrite

Saint Shenoute was born to righteous parents in a village near Akhmim in Upper Egypt, in the year 348 AD. He went on to become the father of thousands of monks, and was known as the Archimandrite.

From a young age, Shenoute had a great love for spending time in prayer, and his father, who was a farmer, had hired a shepherd to care for his sheep. As Shenoute grew up, he also assisted the shepherd. The shepherd was instructed to send Shenoute back every evening before sunset. However, he would always arrive home much later than the appointed time. His parents would get upset with the shepherd for making him come home late, however the shepherd would argue that he had sent him on time. One day the shepherd followed Shenoute on his way home to determine what the cause of his daily delay on the way home was. He found that Shenoute was praying in a nearby water cistern, and found his fingers alight during prayer. When the shepherd saw Shenoute's parents he said, "Take your son. I am not worthy for him to work with me"

Abba Shenoute the Archimandrite

Other Names Saint Shenoute the Great

Birth 348 AD

Feast July 14/Abib 7 (departure)

Famous Quote "If we are sinning in this lifetime, in which lifetime will we do good?"

At the age of nine, his father presented him to Saint Pigol, Saint Shenoute's maternal uncle, to be a monk with him in his monastery, today's Red Monastery in Sohag, which was established on a similar order to that of the Pachomian Koinonia. Upon seeing the young Shenoute, Saint Pigol took the boy's hand and put it upon his own head in order to be blessed by him after being given the prophecy of how great this saint would be. By divine revelation, he placed the schema (the monastic garments) on him ordaining him a monk.

Upon Saint Pigol's departure from this world, Saint Shenoute became the new abbot of the monastery. By the time of his departure in 466 AD, the number of inhabitants had risen to 2,200 monks and 1,800 nuns which required the building of additional houses for monks and separate houses for nuns.

Saint Shenoute along with Saint Pachomious, are considered among the most important leaders of Egyptian coenobitic monasticism (which places emphasis on community life). Those who wished to enter the monastery had to renounce all their belongings and to make a vow, which was introduced by Saint Shenoute, to lead a pure life. Before they were finally accepted, they had to spend a trial period at the gate house, which was also the place where visitors were received, and which was supervised by a trusted monk. Once in the monastery, they were expected to take part in the work and worship of the community. Precise rules regulated all activities, including eating and drinking, which was, of course, severely ascetic. Responsible positions within the monastery were occupied by older, trusted monks.

Saint Shenoute's monastic order placed strong emphasis on the care of the spiritual lives of not only the monks dwelling in the monastery, but also the lay people dwelling in the surrounding villages. He opened the monastery every Saturday and Sunday for those people to provide for not only their physical but also their spiritual needs. His elegant weekly sermons are preserved today and are the sources of spiritual enrichment to all those that read them in addition to being the subjects of several doctoral degrees. Most of his letters, addressed to monks and nuns, deal with monastic questions while others combat pagans and heretics.

Saint Shenoute's wisdom and blessing became increasingly recognised. A constant stream of visitors came to consult with him and to receive his blessing. Bishops and monks would come from across the desert to seek his blessing and advice. Even secular leaders and military commanders would seek his guidance and receive his blessing before going to battle. At that time, he was regarded as one of the great religious leaders of Upper Egypt.

In addition to being a hero of monasticism, he also took great care of the poor. In times of famine, special relief was mounted and the distribution of bread was organized. When an entire village had been plundered by an invading tribe, he took care of it and rebuilt it, and an estimate 20,000 men, women, and children sought refuge behind the walls of the White Monastery. They were fed and clothed by the monks and all their needs were taken care of. Seven monks who had been physicians before consecration tended their sick. 94 people died and were buried; and 52 children were born during their stay at the monastery. Saint Shenoute described this incident in great detail, but was careful not to claim any credit for himself, but rather to praise God who had made this feat possible.

Saint Shenoute provided for us an example of the need for retreat. Despite his heavy responsibilities in the monastery, he withdrew from time to time to the desert, to pray and enjoy a closer communion with God, and it is reported that he was granted visions of our Lord Jesus Christ and many saints.

Because of his popularity in Upper Egypt and his zeal for orthodoxy, Saint Shenoute was chosen by Saint Cyril the Great to accompany him in representing the Church of Alexandria at the Ecumenical Council of Ephesus in 431 AD. There he helped in defeating the heresy of Nestorius, who made a division in the True Union of the divinity and humanity of our Lord Jesus Christ. Because of Saint Shenoute's influence in the territory surrounding his monastery, Nestorius was eventually exiled to Akhmim where he would not be able to sway the true and steadfast faith of those dwelling there. It was at this Ecumenical Council that Saint Shenoute was ordained "Archimandrite." It was revealed from his childhood that he was to be an archimandrite.

Abba Wissa, the disciple of St Shenoute who also became a saint, retold the following story: "*It happened one day that our Saviour was sitting talking with my father Abba Shenoute, and I, Wissa, his disciple, came in wanting to meet him. The Saviour immediately withdrew. After I had come in and received a blessing from my father, I asked him: 'My holy father, who was that talking with you, and where did he go when I came in?' Abba Shenoute said to me: 'It was the Lord Jesus Christ who was with me just now, speaking mysteries to me'. I said to him; 'I, too, would like to see Him so that He might bless me'. My father said to me: 'You will not be able to see him because you are only a novice'. I said to him: 'I am a sinner, my holy father'. He said to me: 'It is not so, but you are faint-hearted'. Again, in tears, I said to him: 'I beg you, my father, let your mercy come upon me so that I, too, may be worthy to see him'. My father said to me: 'If you wait until the sixth hour tomorrow, come in then, and you will find me sitting down with Him. See that you say nothing at all!' On the following day, I came in accordance with my father's instruction and knocked on the door so that I might go in and receive a blessing. Straightaway, the Lord departed from him. I wept and said: 'I am wholly unworthy to see the Lord in the flesh'. But my father said to me: 'He will comfort your heart Wissa, my son and let you hear His sweet voice'. And that one time, though it was more than I deserved, I heard Him speaking with my father, and I have been grateful to him all the days of my life."*

After a long, blessed life of 118 years, he was called upon by our Creator to join the honoured hosts of God's saints in paradise. The Coptic Orthodox Church commemorates this blessed event on the 7th day of the Coptic month of Abib (July 14). His life was documented by the hand of Abba Wissa his disciple.

Saint Abba Wissa

Abba Wissa is most renowned as the disciple of Saint Abba Shenoute and for recounting his life story after his departure. He was born to a rich, pious Christian family.

His father helped the poor celebrate the 3 feasts each Coptic month of Archangel Michael on the 12th, St Mary on the 21st and Annunciation, birth and Resurrection on the 29th.

Abba Wissa

Feast August 10/Mesra 4
(departure)

When he was five years old, Wissa started learning the church books and Holy Bible. He attended church regularly and grew rapidly in wisdom. He had a strong desire to enter monastic life and prayed fervently to the Lord to make it so.

His father knew of his desire and took him to Abba Shenoute. While they were on the way, an angel of the Lord appeared to Abba Shenoute and told him to accept Wissa. He told him that Wissa would become his obedient and private disciple for the rest of his days.

Abba Shenoute accepted him with open arms and Wissa grew in virtue and righteous monastic life. The Lord Jesus then appeared to Abba Shenoute and told him it was time to take Wissa as his own private disciple. Wissa was supported by the Lord in all he did, just like Saint Joseph the Righteous. Abba Wissa knew many of Abba Shenoute's struggles and the Lord Jesus Christ Himself gave Abba Wissa many revelations.

In a revelation to Abba Shenoute, The Lord Jesus told him, *"Send your son Wissa with some monks to Abba Macari, the Bishop of Edko (near the monastery) to help him. The pagans had tied him up and his disciples and they are getting ready to offer them as a sacrifice to the idols."*

Abba Wissa went immediately on the way to the temple of idols but found the doors locked. They prayed, and the doors were opened. This frightened the pagans who released Bishop Macari immediately as well as his disciples. They prayed together and fire came down from heaven and burnt the idols with their priests.

Saint Shenoute tried to appoint Abba Wissa as his successor but he refused. Saint Shenoute then insisted that this was the Lord's command to which he then accepted out of obedience.

He guided and strengthened the monks for 20 years as Abbot of the monastery after the departure of Saint Shenoute. He was a profound writer and wrote the biography of Saint Shenoute among many other works, some of which can still be found among "the collection of Karzoun" in the Bristish Museum.

He departed in peace on the 4th day of the Coptic month of Misra.

PART 5
MODERN DAY SAINTS

SAINT ANBA ABRAAM
Bishop of Fayoum and Giza

Anba Abraam, known as 'the friend of the poor', was born in 1829 A.D. in the village of Gelda in Minya. He was named Boules (Paul) Ghobrial by his parents, who were righteous and loved God.

He received his education at the church school, where he was also taught about the Holy Bible, psalms and praises. At the age of eight, his mother departed.

Abba Abraam

Other Names Friend of the poor

Birth 1892 AD

Feast Baouna 3 / June 10 (departure)

Soon after, at the age of fifteen, he was ordained as a deacon by Bishop Youssab after he was recommended by the village priests. He yearned for monastic life and at the age of nineteen he was ordained a monk at the El-Muharraq Monastery of St. Mary and took the name of Father Boules El-Muharraqy.

He was known for his patience and self-control, and his interest in almsgiving. Anba Yakoubos the Bishop heard about him and asked him to come to the 'Bishop's House' and remain with him. Father Boules went and worked day and night and changed the 'Bishop's house' to a shelter for the poor. His deep eagerness for the life of ascetism caused him to ask the Bishop to allow him to leave for the monastery again after he spent four years helping him.

The Bishop then ordained him as a priest and allowed him to return to the monastery in 1863. The monks then elected him to overseer of the monastery. He opened the doors of the monastery to the poor. A lot of young men heard about him and came to him asking him to teach them and there was shortly forty new monks ordained. He remained the Abbot of the monastery for five years, during which time, the monastery was the refuge for thousands of the poor, hence his title became, *the father of the poor and destitute.* Also, during his time as the Abbot, he did not spare an effort to improve the condition of the monastery spiritually and physically. He improved its finances by developing its agricultural land.

After five years of this blessed service, as he increased his charity toward the poor, the orphans and the widows, the devil became infuriated and made some of the monks think that Father Boules' charitable works were wasting the money of the monastery and so they complained against him to Anba Morcos, Metropolitan of El-Behira. In 1870, Father Boules was asked to leave the monastery. Father Boules did not argue, and left El-Muharraq monastery and went to the monastery of El-Baramous accompanied by several monks. One of the monks who wanted to leave with him was Father Mikhail El-Beheiry, his famous disciple; however Father Boules insisted that he should stay at the monastery as a source of blessing for the place and to continue in charitable deeds.

Father Boules devoted all his time to prayer and studying the Bible, but his deep love for the poor people did not end. He loved the hostile Arabs (Bedouins) who were living in the area of the monastery and he shared with them everything he had, even his clothes.

In 1881 A.D. (1597 A.M.), Pope Kyrillos V chose Father Boules and ordained him a Bishop for the parish of El-Fayoum and El-Giza to replace its reposed Bishop, Anba Eisak. Father Boules was ordained with the name of Anba Abraam. During his time as a Bishop (1881 -1914 A.D.), the episcopate became a place of rest and comfort for the poor and rich alike.

He became famous for two attributes;

First, his charity to the multitude of poor that came to the Bishopric residence. He gave them all what he had of money. He made the Bishopric residence a shelter for many of them. He offered clothing for those who had no clothes and food for those who were hungry. He never allowed anyone to offer him food that was better than that offered to the poor. Once he went down to visit the poor while they were eating, and found that the food he was offered that day was better than that offered to them. He became very sad, and immediately relieved the nun supervising the feeding service of the poor from her duties.

Second, he was famous for his faith filled prayers. Many miracles were performed through his prayers. His fame spread to all parts of Egypt and even to some parts of Europe. Many patients of different religions came to him, seeking the blessing of his prayers and were healed. He also had great knowledge of the holy books, and his depth of knowledge was manifest in the advice, instructions and sermons that he gave. More importantly, he possessed a pure nature and many virtues, particularly, his severe denial of himself, and his true renouncement of the pleasures of life and its vain glory. His food and clothing were merely the bare necessities. He was also straightforward in revealing his own opinion, looking only for the truth. He never gave any attention to the rank and greatness of people in higher places, for their greatness was far less than the greatness of the truth. It was said that other priests and bishops feared him because of this.

It happened that Anba Abraam received furniture for the episcopate. He refused to use it, and asked one of the servants to put it in storage. When a woman approached him about her inability to buy the furniture needed for the wedding of her daughter, he gave her everything. Some of the people complained to Pope Kyrillos V about giving away the furniture. Afterwards, there was a collection to build a new house of the episcopate. Anba Abraam gave that money also to the poor and the needy, so the people made another complaint. The Pope summoned him, and he went without delay. It was a summer afternoon, he walked in, the shutters were closed and there was a ray of the sun through a hole in the shade of the window. Anba Abraam was then very old, he mistook the light beam for a laundry robe, it was a common practice to have a laundry robe for hanging clothes. He threw his overcoat on the beam and the coat stayed there! The Pope, seeing how the Lord worked wonders to support and not embarrass this saint on earth, changed the purpose of the call, and instead inquired about his health and later gave him 15,000 Egyptian Pounds to build a new house for the episcopate.

When the people came back to see the Pope, he rebuked them for their lack of faith, saying, *"How can I argue with a man of God who was able to hang his coat on a ray of the sun?"* The new house of the episcopate was not built in Anba Abraam's lifetime. The money was again used to help the poor.

He was a scholar in the Holy Bible studies. He learned the extracts by heart and repeated them from memory. This was a result of his studying the Scriptures at the Monastery of El-Baramous. Some monks said that he read the whole Bible every forty days. It is said that he used to collect his people every evening for prayers, and gave someone the responsibility for reading many chapters of the Bible, and then he would explain them. He encouraged the priests and preachers to deliver sermons, and he himself used to attend those meetings, and to comment on anything wrong they might say concerning the dogma or the rites of the church.

One day, a poor woman went to him when the Bishop had no money. But someone had given him a shawl, which he never used. He apologized to the woman that he had no money, and gave her the shawl saying that she may sell it and use the money. The woman took it and went to the market to sell it. There the owner of the shawl saw her, bought it from her and returned it to the Bishop. Before giving the shawl to the Bishop, he asked, *"Father why did you not use the shawl as it is cold these days?"* The Bishop replied, *"The shawl is Upstairs my son"* meaning that it is with the Lord Jesus Christ. Then the man presented the shawl to him. The Bishop said,

"I hope you gave the poor woman the right price." The man replied, *"Yes father, I gave her the right price."*

One well known story is told about three young men who plotted to take advantage of the Bishop's love for the poor. Two of them approached the Bishop saying that the third had died, and that they had nothing to bury him. The Bishop nodded his head, and gave them an offering saying, *"Take it and bury him..."* They left laughing, but they were astonished to find that their friend had actually died. They tried to return the money asking the Bishop for forgiveness. He forgave them but did not accept the money, telling them to bury their friend with it.

Anba Abraam spent 33 years as Bishop. He had a life of intimate communion with our Lord Jesus Christ and his saints. He enjoyed the liturgy with all the hymns and praises, and he lived a life of extreme monasticism. He chose poverty, and was extremely generous, loving, and kind to the poor.

In his final days on earth, he was bed ridden for one month, and a multitude of people went to see him and receive his blessings. He informed those who were close to him that he was going away to be with the Lord Jesus Christ. On the 3rd day of Baouna, Anba Abraam, the Friend of the Poor departed to heaven. More than ten thousand Christians and Muslims walked in his funeral procession. To this day, his pure body is laid in a tomb that was prepared for him in the Church of the monastery of the Virgin Mary in El-Fayoum.

In 1964, The Holy Synod of the Coptic Orthodox Patriarchate of Alexandria canonized Bishop Abraam as a saint.

Father Mikhail El-Beheiry

Father Mikhail El-Beheiry was born in the year 1847AD to righteous parents in El-Minya Governorate, Egypt.

Since his early childhood he used to lean towards solitude and meditation. His father departed when he was 12 years old. He contemplates on his father's departure saying, "*While sitting there all by myself, I saw my father's soul ascending to heaven accompanied by angels and heavenly hosts. I called him, "My father, my father", but the angels said to me, "Pray that your end would be like your father's", then they disappeared and I could see them no more.*"

Three or four years later his mother also passed away, thus he enjoyed repeating with the Psalmist, "*When my father and my mother forsake me, then the Lord will take care of me*" (Ps. 27: 10).

A big project was launched to build some small bridges in the village and all the residents had to participate, and this saint was one of them. Once they had finished, he and his friend were

Fr Mikhail El-Beheiry

Other Names man of kindness, father of the needy

Birth 1847 AD

Feast Amsheer 16/ February 23 (departure)

Famous Quote "A person who is praying should have total faith that the Lord is hearing his/her prayer "He who planted the ear, shall He not hear?" {Ps. 94: 9}, otherwise he/she is praying in vain."

True prayer puts you in the most sublime spiritual situation, it lifts you up to be standing before the Lord and talking to Him."

walking back home in the dark. As it was a dark night, they lost their way and instead, they passed through a deserted area, which people always avoided going through because of two fierce hyenas living there. As soon as they saw the hyenas, his friend was about to faint, yet the saint thought they were two dogs and calmed his friend. To his friend's astonishment, he saw the two hyenas yielding to the saint as friends. The hyenas walked with them, and he was talking to them thinking they were dogs, till they reached the city borders, where the guarding dogs smelled the hyenas approaching and started to bark and howl. The residents thought there was something serious happening and they all got their weapons and came out ready for any danger. When they learnt the truth they were amazed and glorified the Lord in His saints.

At the age of 20, he abandoned the world and headed to Al Muharraq Monastery. This was at the time when Fr Boules (later Anba Abraam) was there. After 18 months as a novice, he was ordained as a monk with 39 other novices.

In 1870, some troubles started in the Monastery, which resulted in banishing Father Boules the Abbot (Anba Abraam) who left accompanied by a number of monks who insisted to go with him. When they asked Father Mikhail to go with them, Father Boules said: "*Let him stay in the Monastery so that the men of God would still be living here, lest the wrath of God would come upon this place. His presence in the Monastery comforts us.*"

Father Mikhail faced persecution from those around him in the Monastery. One time while he was baking the holy bread, one of the monks secretly went to Father Mikhail's cell, took all his clothes and belongings and left. After he finished baking, the saint went back to his cell to change his dirty and wet clothes but he found nothing. In his distress, as it was a freezing cold winter day and he needed to change, he went to Father Mikhail of Abu Tig, who succeeded Father Boules as the Abbot. He told him what had happened hoping that he would even give him a garment to change; but on the contrary, he rebuked him saying: "*Did you reach that extent of boldness and rudeness to accuse your fellow monks of stealing from your cell?*" Although he didn't accuse any one, he just reported the loss of his belongings. Father Mikhail El-Beheiry left repeating with Job the Righteous: "*The Lord gave, and the Lord has taken away; Blessed be the name of the Lord.*" (Job 1: 20). Telling his confession father Hegumen Saleeb Al Alony about what had happened, he gave him a shawl made of harsh sack cloth; which he kept wearing all winter, he couldn't even wash it because that was the only thing to wear. They did lots of similar incidents to annoy him and make him leave the Monastery. Father Mikhail was always silent and lived in total humility tolerating whatever happened to him. He never let go of his patience and counted these persecutions as a basic means of salvation. He accepted all sorts of humiliation in dignity and honour, which helped him to rise to higher spiritual levels and new heights in spiritual warfare.

After the departure of Fr Mikhail of Abu Tig who was the abbot of the monastery for 14 years, he was succeeded by Hegumen Saleeb who was one of Anba Abraam's disciples. During this time, Fr Mikhail El-Beheiry started covering the old books in the Monastery with leather covers to preserve them from damage. Monks and laymen used to come asking him to do the same for old books they had, firstly to have his blessings and secondly, according to their wish, to give him some money for covering their books. He accepted the money for a very noble reason: to help the many poor and needy people around him. His virtues started to be clear to everyone and they all smelled the sweet aroma of the Lord Jesus in our blessed saint.

When Bishop Sawiros of Sanabo and Qusqam visited Al Muharraq Monastery in 1874AD, he ordained Father Mikhail as a priest, after recommendation from the abott and rest of the monks. Father Mikhail became increasingly respected because of his numerous virtues: asceticism, continuous fasting, chastity and humility. He became a confession father for many clergymen and laymen alike. He accepted them all, guided them and advised in great love. People felt so comforted and relaxed after sitting with him, as if a huge burden was lifted off their shoulders.

All the donations which came to the Monastery especially during feasts and special occasions, were appropriately distributed according to the church's needs, concerning candles, oils and other different departments. Many people came from everywhere to meet him and have his blessings. They brought many gifts and donations, which he wisely dealt with. He used to give the poor and needy from the donations of clothes and money, and then would give the rest to the Abbot to use as he wished. He kept very little for his urgent needs and wouldn't let the money stay with him for a long time for fear of the tricks of the devil.

He was called by everyone '*The man of kindness and the father of the needy,*' as he supported many laymen and colleague monks. He was a copy of his father, the charitable and merciful, Anba Abraam of Fayoum and Giza.

He loved his handiwork and it is said that when he was a youth, he planted a small garden and would spend hours looking after it during his free time. He would do this to avoid over-sleeping and giving his body rest, and in his mercy, gave his brother monks some fruit to eat in his mercy.

It happened that the trees and palms in this garden had to be cut off when renovating and building new cells in the Monastery, but he was never troubled or got sad. When asked about this issue, he answered: "*Why do you think I would get upset? When I started this garden the aim was to praise the Lord, so the same aim is still present even after cutting the fruit trees and palms. Praise is due to our Lord at all times. I had planted this garden to work and be able to resist the devils' fights because they launch wars with idol monks who are not doing enough work, but if the devil starts fighting me now with anger, sadness, distress and pain for cutting the trees and depriving me of my garden, then I would calm myself down saying: people would always remember and praise me for that garden, so now it is gone, I have to look up towards heaven and do good deeds to dwell in the everlasting Paradise.*"

He used to fast daily till sunset, then eat very little together with praying continuously day and night. He didn't eat meat from the day of his ordination as a monk till his departure, yet he never announced his fasting. For example if he was visiting someone and they offered him a cup of coffee, he would take it, but if they offered him food, he would claim that he was still full from breakfast or lunch, and added: "*but I don't want to upset you my son… I'll take a little bit,*" after having a little bit he would have a sip of water.

He was highly renowned for his arrow prayers and emphasised the importance of prayer. He instructed people to "*hold fast to the virtue of true prayer and you can guarantee salvation.*"

He always encouraged the monks to come to his cell and read whatever spiritual books they wanted, or to talk to him saying, "*My children, the door of my cell is always opened, you are most welcome to come any time, don't think you are interrupting me, but be sure that whoever comes to hear the life-giving word of God will do me a favour because then I don't have to worry about you and come to find you, so you are giving me a rest.*"

Father Mikhail lost his sight as he grew older, and although he suffered a lot of troubles as a result, he still thanked God continually and continued in patience. He used to comfort himself saying: "*Other creatures such as the flies and ants share human beings in having the sense of the sight, but as we are God's speaking creation we are given the great gift of mind, through which we can see God with faith. With this spiritual sight we see the Kingdom of Heaven.*"

If I am driven from my physical sight, I plead the Lord not to be driven from enjoying the Divine Light. Oh! I deserve it because of my many sins. I thank my Lord and ask Him to pour His mercies that I may rejoice more and more."

At the village of Beni Rafe there was a sorcerer, and once a group of friends gathered in his house and asked him to prove his professionalism and send one of his spiritual helpers to Father Mikhail's cell to who was visiting him and promised him a large sum of money if he carried out their request! They didn't inform the sorcerer about who Father Mikhail El-Beheiry was or any of his virtues as a holy man. Sending one of his devilish helpers, he came back frightened and shaking saying: *"I can go around the entire land and do whatever you ask me to do, but I can never come close to Father Mikhail's cell at all, because every time I tried to do so, I found it surrounded by blazing fire that prevented me from entering."*

Father Mikhail was very well known for his spiritual education, eloquence and convincing answers. In 1920 and 1921 the honourable deacon Saint Habib Girgis visited the monastery, and after spending some time with Father Mikhail he told everyone about the depth of his knowledge and spirituality. He visited Father Mikhail daily during the period of his stay in the monastery.

Father Mikhail died at the age of 76, 56 years after he left the world and joined the monastery. He departed on the 16th of Amsheer in 1693 AM (23rd February 1923 AD). After two weeks of his departure, three people saw light coming out of his tomb. Those people knew nothing about the saint, but when they reported seeing the light they were informed that Father Mikhail El Beheiry had departed two weeks ago and that was his tomb.

SAINT POPE KYRILLOS VI

St. Pope Kyrillos (Cyril) VI was the 117th Pope of Alexandria and Patriarch of the See of St Mark. Pope Kyrillos sat on the throne of St Mark for twelve years (1959-1971). The church commemorates his feast on March 9.

Pope Kyrillos was born on August 2nd 1902 as Azer Ata. He was raised in a loving Christian family, who taught him the love of God, the life of prayer and the practice of the Holy Liturgy. From a very young age, Pope Kyrillos enjoyed the time he spent in the presence of God, and desired a monastic life: *"When I grew up, I heard much about monks, and my heart was filled with a deep longing to join the monastery."*

While still being a lay person, Pope Kyrillos practised a highly virtuous life, and as such his monastic path was a continuation of a high degree of Christian living, rather than the start of it. He was a strong believer in a lay person being able to attain a high level of spirituality, even higher than some of the celibates.

One virtue practised by the Pope as a lay person was the virtue

Pope Kyrillos VI

Other Names Friend of the poor

Birth August 2, 1902

Feast Amshir 30/ March 9 (departure)

Famous Quote Anyone who sits in seclusion and reads his Psalms is like a man who sees the King. Also, he who sits in seclusion and cries over his sins, is like a man who speaks to the King of morning metanias (prostrations): *"When you awake, do not remain in bed. Make the sign of the cross on your face, stand up and pray the Our Father. Start your day worshipping God in prostration, twenty or thirty times, or as many times as possible: for among all other practices undertaken by people, there is none better than this one."* Later on as a pope, he would reflect on his time as a layperson, and admonish his younger disciples by saying, *"Remember Your creator in the days of your youth."*

At a young age, Pope Kyrillos left the world, and headed to the monastery of El-Baramous. In a later letter to one of his disciples, this joy is expressed: *"The day I forsook the world was the happiest day of my life. When I entered the monastery, I felt like I walked into the Garden of Eden, and the monks were like angels."* After a short probation period, he was ordained a monk on the feast day of St Mina, and so to his great delight, the fathers decided to name him Fr Mina the Monk.

Pope Kyrillos lived many years of his monastic life in solitude, initially in a cave two miles away from the monastery, and then later in a deserted windmill south of Cairo. The devil tried to frighten him from the life of solitude: *"During my stay in the cave, I met with several wars and opposition from the devil. It is difficult for me to describe what happened during my first night there. I felt that the enemy had gathered all his forces to battle against a weak man like myself. I was filled with fear, as I heard terrible sounds and fearful quakes. But with God's care, I was encouraged."*

He describes this time as some of the most joyful periods of his life, as he was allowed more than ever to enjoy the presence of God. During his time in the windmill, he followed a strict spiritual canon, including Tasbeha each morning at 4am, a daily liturgy, metanias and a strict fasting regiment. Pope Kyrillos recited the prayers of the Agpia, as well as personal prayers throughout the day. His prayers were often accompanied by tears. He often taught the importance of spending quiet time with God: *"Anyone who sits in seclusion and reads his Psalms is like a man who sees the King. Also, he who sits in seclusion and cries over his sins, is like a man who speaks to the King."*

He always taught his disciples, *"you should pray softly to God."* As a result of living continually in God's presence, Pope Kyrillos was always at comfort, no matter the challenges he faced: *"At all times I have a continuous flow of comfort and blessing. The Lord's grace flutters its wings, and casts away any trouble or sadness, and heals the heart with its indescribable balm. Oh how sweet it is to feel this in your heart. When a man is sad, troubled or discouraged, He hurries to comfort and encourage him. How great and abundant are the mercies and blessings God gave man to enjoy."*

In April 1959, after the departure of Pope Yosab, Pope Kyrillos was elected Pope and Patriarch of the See of St Mark. During his papacy, many were attracted to the monastic life after seeing his sincere example. He encouraged all believers to pursue a higher level of spirituality, and to enjoy the blessing of continual prayer, even whilst at work, or whilst undertaking their daily duties. *"From time to time, while you are at work, you can say O My Lord Jesus Christ help me – the name of Jesus is the sword with which we can torment our enemies."* He also taught us the reliance on God in all things. One of his most famous sayings was: *"Do not be concerned, trust the Lord! Have you known anyone who trusted in God and was let down? Heaven forbid!"*

Pope Kyrillos himself had a huge reliance on God in all aspects of his life, especially the affairs of the church. At times, he faced much opposition from church administrators for not spending enough time on church affairs, and choosing rather to maintain a highly spiritual timetable, including a daily mass. However, the truth was that his reliance was on God, and God always sorted out the church affairs in miraculous ways. In one of his letters to a spiritual son, he writes: *"Do not reflect much on the affairs of life. Do not worry about anything. Cast your burdens upon the Lord, and He shall sustain you."*

As a result of his very strict spiritual canon, Pope Kyrillos was known as the *"Man of Prayer."* For over thirty-five years, he celebrated the Holy liturgy daily. Though approaching the age of seventy, he still woke up daily at 4am to start his daily prayers, and pray a liturgy. Pope Kyrillos recognized the importance of a daily liturgy, and insisted on praying the Divine Liturgy and receiving Holy Communion daily, regardless of any difficulties or obstacles to this.

He had a strong belief in the power of the liturgy in his life: *"In all that you require, supplicate the Lord with unceasing prayers during the Liturgy, for this is an opportune time. It is during the Liturgy that the doors of heaven are open. It is the time that Christ is present among us, offering His flesh and blood in Holy Communion, so that we may live and be granted the forgiveness of our sins."*

God granted Pope Kyrillos the spiritual gift of performing miracles. Thousands of miracles both during his life, and even after his departure, have been recorded in books. His spirituality led him to have the ability to predict future events, heal diseases, and cast out demons. During the time of final examinations, thousands of students came to him for his prayers and blessings. It is said that most Coptic people living at the time of Pope Kyrillos had either witnessed a miracle in their own lives through his prayers, or at least had seen one in someone close to them.

Pope Kyrillos had a very special relationship with his intercessor, St Mina, and would often call Saint Mina for help in difficult times. Pope Kyrillos built the first monastery of Saint Mina, and the first bishop he ordained was with the name Mina. Every year he would celebrate the feast of St Mina with a joyful spirit." Pope Shenouda commented once: "I wonder when Pope Kyrillos' soul meets Saint Mina's how they will greet each other! He never loved any saint more than Mari Mina."

After faithfully looking after the Church, Pope Kyrillos departed to heaven on March 9, 1971. Initially he was buried under the Altar in the Coptic Cathedral in Cairo, but after Pope Shenouda read his will, he discovered that he had wished to be buried at the Monastery of his patron saint, and close friend, Saint Mina. His body remains there till this day.

At his funeral, Pope Shenouda III gave a eulogy about this great saint, and concluded by saying: "Every virtuous *trait available could be found in Pope Kyrillos*." His example teaches us many virtues including;

- Regular attendance of the Holy Liturgy

- Knowing that the Heavens are open to our requests

- Relying on God

- Having an intercessor

- The practise of continual prayer

- Spending quiet time in the presence of God

- Continually striving for higher spiritual levels.

Saint Habib Girgis

Habib Kozman Mankarious Girgis was born to Christian parents in 1876. He is most renowned for his influence on religious education in the Coptic church, having founded Sunday school as a part of the liturgical life of young Christians. He was the dean of the modern day Catechetical School of Alexandria. He was canonised a saint on June 20, 2013.

At the age of six, his father passed away. His family endured much financial hardships. Alas, Habib was able to complete primary school and started going to a reputable secondary school. He finished secondary school with honours. While most children of the time would consider it a great success to complete secondary education, Habib Girgis completed and excelled in his studies.

St Habib Girgis

Other Names Friend of the poor

Birth 1876 AD

Feast August 21, 1951

Habib Girgis was then one of twelve students to join the Clerical College. There was no teacher of religion for four years but this did not stand in his way. He spent hours at the Patriarchal Library. Habib became a self-educated theologian. He was even asked to teach the other students.

The Clerical College was in much need of a building, so Pope Cyril V sent Habib to the churches to give sermons. Many were moved by his words and made financial contributions to the building of the Clerical College.

Habib Girgis could see that there was a deficit in the Coptic education system. A deficit that Protestant and Catholic ministries were excelling in for years. Protestant and Catholics began to influence poorly educated Copts. This was compounded by the low levels of literacy that existed among the Coptic people and even clergy. The children were not being taught any forms of religious education and had no set athletic or social gatherings. Habib Girgis saw a need to educate the entire church so that they could defend and remain steadfast in their faith.

His vision for the Coptic church was to improve academic standards across the country. Habib established Sunday school in the major cities of Egypt. This was received with great interest by young Coptic children and thus, became the main pillar of revolution of Coptic Orthodox Christianity till this day.

By 1899, Pope Cyril V issued an official decree that all Coptic children should attend Sunday school. By the early 1900s, Sunday School was flourishing around Coptic churches. This was at a time when public schooling was established in Egypt.

His contributions and tireless efforts compelled Pope Cyril V to ordain him Archdeacon in 1918. His life was completely devoted to increasing education in the church. He was a talented orator and communicated in a way that united the members of the church.

By 1949, 43 000 children were being taught Christian religious education by 2 500 teachers. The movement expanded to include youth and adults as well.

He departed in 1951 at the age of 75. On June 20, 2013, under the Patriarchy of HH Pope Tawadros II, Habib Girgis was canonised, Saint Habib Girgis.